Easy
Beading

Fast. Fashionable. Fun.

Vol. 5

The best projects from the fifth year of *BeadStyle* magazine

KALMBACH BOOKS

Kalmbach Books

21027 Crossroads Circle
Waukesha, Wisconsin 53186
www.Kalmbach.com/books

Published in 2009

13 12 11 10 09   1 2 3 4 5

Printed in China

ISBN: 978-0-87116-288-5

Visit our Web site at
BeadAndCraftBooks.com
Secure online ordering available

Publisher's Cataloging-In-Publication Data

Easy beading. Vol. 5 : fast, fashionable, fun : the best projects from the fifth year of *BeadStyle* magazine.

  p., : col. ill. ; cm.

  All projects have appeared previously in *BeadStyle* magazine.
  Includes index.
  ISBN: 978-0-87116-288-5

1. Beadwork–Handbooks, manuals, etc. 2. Beads–Handbooks, manuals, etc. 3. Jewelry making–Handbooks, manuals, etc.
I. Title: *BeadStyle* Magazine.

TT860 .E29 2009
745.594/2

Contents

COVER PAGE 104
Photo taken by Jim Forbes

26

14 Crystals

55

46 Gemstones

76

82 Mixed Media

113

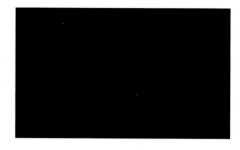

138 Glass

153

180 Metal & Chain

194

208 Pearls

221

Introduction

BeadStyle magazine celebrated its fifth anniversary in September 2008. This fifth volume of *Easy Beading* celebrates the beautiful work of that year — I see it as sort of an anniversary party photo album marking a great celebration.

It's amazing how much has changed in beading in such a short time. Making stylish jewelry used to be a more expensive proposition than it is today. Everything was about gemstones and fine metals. Don't get me wrong — I love gemstones and sterling silver, but it's wonderful to have a wider range of style, material and price options.

There are so many beautiful and fashionable types of chain and findings available in base metals today. And gorgeous beads can be found in every material in the world — even gemstones are easier to find — at better prices.

The reason? There are so many more, great local and online bead stores than there were when *BeadStyle* started. And big craft chains are carrying more and better beading materials. It's a great time to be a beader!

You'll see examples of many terrific options on the following pages. As in previous volumes, we've organized this fifth volume of *Easy Beading* by materials used: crystals, gemstones, mixed media, glass, metal & chain, and pearls. Check your local bead store and craft store first for supplies. We've provided specific information for unique items for your convenience.

While the name of the book is *Easy Beading*, as always, it includes projects

for a range of skill levels. (Look for the half circle at the top of the page to find projects specifically for beginners.) And we know that while your style and creativity are limitless, your time — like your budget — is not. You can make any of these projects in a just a couple of hours or less.

I hope you enjoy them as much as we did.
Warmest regards,

Cathy

CATHY JAKICIC,
EDITOR, *BEADSTYLE* MAGAZINE
editor@beadstylemag.com

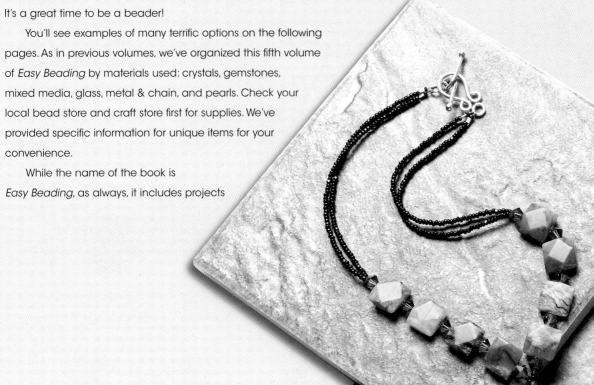

Beader's Glossary

A visual reference to common beads and findings

gemstone shapes

| lentil | rondelle | faceted rondelle | round | oval | marquise | rectangle |

| tube | briolette | teardrop | chips | nugget |

---

crystal and glass

| Czech fire-polished | bicone | top-drilled bicone | cube | oval | drop |

| briolette | cone | round | saucer | top-drilled saucer (with jump ring) |

| flat back | rhinestone rondelle | rhinestone squaredelle | dichroic |

lampworked   yo yo   glass flowers   leaves   dagger

teardrop   fringe drops   seed beads   triangle   cube   bugle

pearls, shells, and miscellaneous

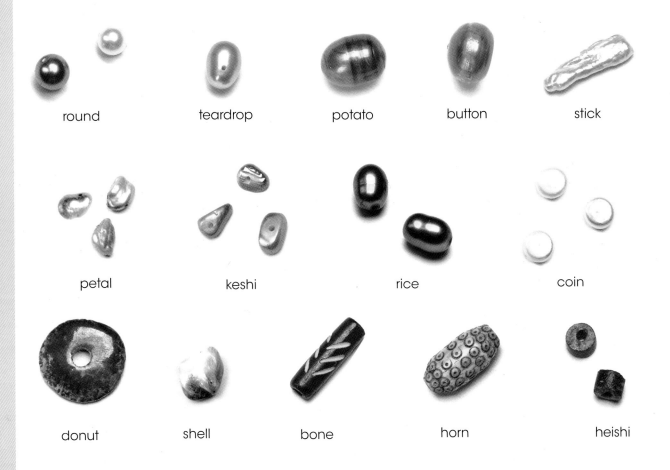

round   teardrop   potato   button   stick

petal   keshi   rice   coin

donut   shell   bone   horn   heishi

findings, spacers, and connectors

French hook
ear wires

post earring
finding

hoop earring

lever-back
earring finding

ear
thread

magnetic
clasp

S-hook
clasp

lobster claw
clasp

toggle
clasp

two-strand
toggle clasp

box
clasp

slide
clasp

hook-and-eye
clasps

snap
clasp

pinch crimp
end

crimp
ends

coil end

crimp cone

tube bail
with loop

tube-shaped
and round crimp
beads

crimp
covers

bead tips

jump rings and
soldered jump
rings

split ring

spacers

bead
caps

pinch bail

caterpillar

multistrand
spacer bars

two-strand
curved tube

single-strand
tube

3-to-1 and 2-to-1
connectors

5-to-1 chandelier
component

bail

cone

tools, stringing materials, and chain

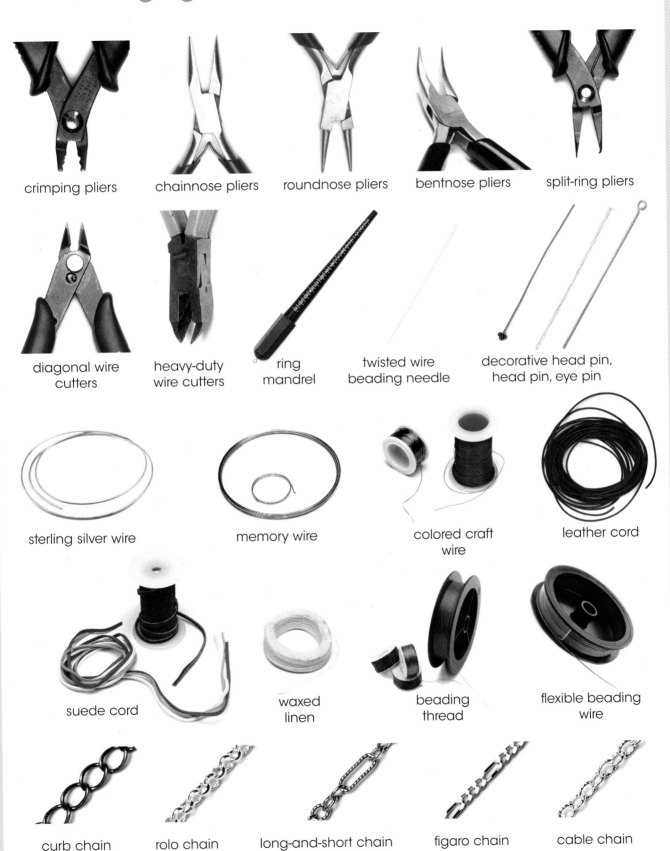

crimping pliers

chainnose pliers

roundnose pliers

bentnose pliers

split-ring pliers

diagonal wire cutters

heavy-duty wire cutters

ring mandrel

twisted wire beading needle

decorative head pin, head pin, eye pin

sterling silver wire

memory wire

colored craft wire

leather cord

suede cord

waxed linen

beading thread

flexible beading wire

curb chain

rolo chain

long-and-short chain

figaro chain

cable chain

Basics

A step-by-step reference to key jewelry-making techniques used in bead-stringing projects.

plain loop

1

Trim the wire or head pin ⅜ in. (1 cm) above the top bead. Make a right angle bend close to the bead.

2

Grab the wire's tip with round-nose pliers. The tip of the wire should be flush with the pliers. Roll the wire to form a half circle. Release the wire.

3

Reposition the pliers in the loop and continue rolling.

4

The finished loop should form a centered circle above the bead.

wrapped loop

1

Make sure you have at least 1¼ in. (3.2 cm) of wire above the bead. With the tip of your chainnose pliers, grasp the wire directly above the bead. Bend the wire (above the pliers) into a right angle.

2

Using roundnose pliers, position the jaws in the bend as shown.

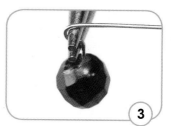

3

Bring the wire over the top jaw of the roundnose pliers.

4

Reposition the pliers' lower jaw snugly into the loop. Curve the wire downward around the bottom of the roundnose pliers. This is the first half of a wrapped loop.

5

To make the second half of the wrapped loop, position the chainnose pliers' jaws across the loop.

6

Wrap the wire around the wire stem, covering the stem between the loop and the top bead. Trim the excess wire and press the cut end close to the wraps with chainnose pliers.

opening and closing loops or jump rings

1

Hold the loop or jump ring with two pairs of chainnose pliers or chainnose and roundnose pliers, as shown.

2

To open the loop or jump ring, bring one pair of pliers toward you and push the other pair away. Reverse the steps to close the open loop or jump ring.

split ring

To open a split ring, slide the hooked tip of split-ring pliers between the two overlapping wires.

surgeon's knot

Cross the right end over the left end and go through the loop. Go through again. Pull the ends to tighten. Cross the left end over the right end and go through once. Pull the ends to tighten.

overhand knot

Make a loop and pass the working end through it. Pull the ends to tighten the knot.

lark's head knot

Fold a cord in half and lay it behind a ring, loop, etc. with the fold pointing down. Bring the ends through the ring from back to front, then through the fold and tighten.

making wraps above a top-drilled bead

1

Center a top-drilled bead on a 3-in. (7.6 cm) piece of wire. Bend each wire upward to form a squared-off U shape.

2

Cross the wires into an X above the bead.

3

Using chainnose pliers, make a small bend in each wire so they form a right angle.

4

Wrap the horizontal wire around the vertical wire as in a wrapped loop. Trim the excess wrapping wire.

folded crimp end

1

Glue one end of the cord and place it in a crimp end. Use chainnose pliers to fold one side of the crimp end over the cord.

2

Repeat on the second side and squeeze gently. Test to be sure the crimp end is secure.

flattened crimp

1

Hold the crimp using the tip of your chainnose pliers. Squeeze the pliers firmly to flatten the crimp.

2

Tug the wire to make sure the crimp has a solid grip. If the wire slides, repeat the steps with a new crimp.

folded crimp

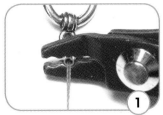

1

Position the crimp bead in the notch closest to the crimping pliers' handle.

2

Separate the wires and firmly squeeze the crimp.

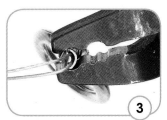

3

Move the crimp into the notch at the pliers' tip and hold the crimp as shown. Squeeze the crimp bead, folding it in half at the indentation.

4

Test that the folded crimp is secure.

cutting flexible beading wire

Decide how long you want your necklace to be. Add 6 in. (15 cm) and cut a piece of beading wire to that length. (For a bracelet, add 5 in./13 cm.)

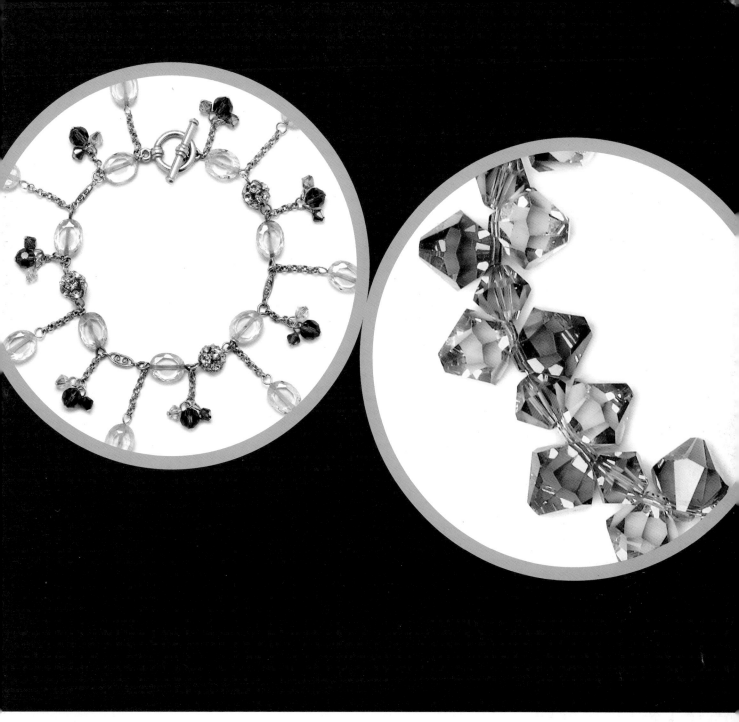

Crystals

Depth of

the blues

by Irina Miech

Use the many blue-crystal options to create a multihued necklace

From azure to ultramarine, the color blue has a broad spectrum all its own. Swarovski alone has more than a dozen different blues. Many people consider blue their favorite color, but which blue? There are so many to choose from. Create your own personal blue palette with this necklace-and-earring set.

1 **necklace** • Arrange three sets of 11 6 mm round crystals in the following color patterns: ABCD, BCDA, CDAB.

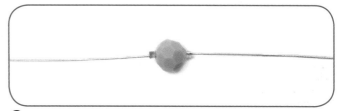

2 **a** Cut a piece of beading wire (Basics, p. 12). Cut two more pieces, each 1 in. (2.5 cm) longer than the previous piece.
   b On the short wire, center a microcrimp bead, the center bead in the first crystal set, and a microcrimp bead. Flatten the microcrimp beads (Basics).

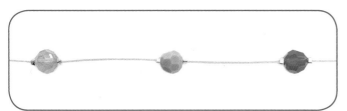

3 **a** On each end, 1 in. (2.5 cm) from the microcrimp, string a microcrimp bead, the next crystal in the sequence, and a microcrimp bead. Flatten the microcrimp beads. Repeat until the strand is within 2 in. (5 cm) of the finished length.
   b Repeat steps 2b and 3a on the medium and long wires with the remaining crystal sets.

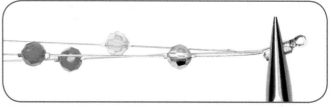

4 On one side, over all three strands, string a crimp end. Adjust the strands so the crystals don't touch. Flatten the crimp end (Basics). Repeat on the other side. Trim the excess wire.

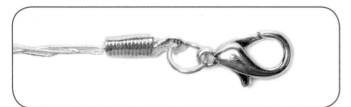

5 Open a jump ring (Basics). Attach a crimp end and a clasp. Close the jump ring. Repeat on the other end, substituting a soldered jump ring for the clasp.

Tip

Because so much of the beading wire is visible, use sterling silver, silver-plated, or silver-colored wire.

1 **earrings** · On an eye pin, string two 6 mm round crystals.

2 Attach a Scrimp to the end of the eye pin, using a Scrimp screwdriver.

3 Open the loop of an earring wire (Basics, p. 12). Attach the dangle. Close the loop. Make a second earring to match the first.

Supplies

necklace (16 in./41 cm)
- ◆ **33–39** 6 mm round crystals, in four colors
- ◆ flexible beading wire, .014 or .015
- ◆ **2** 6 mm jump rings
- ◆ **66–78** microcrimp beads
- ◆ **2** crimp ends
- ◆ lobster claw clasp and soldered jump ring
- ◆ chainnose pliers
- ◆ diagonal wire cutters

earrings
- ◆ **4** 6 mm round crystals
- ◆ **2** 1-in. (2.5 cm) eye pins
- ◆ **2** Scrimps
- ◆ pair of earring wires
- ◆ chainnose pliers
- ◆ Scrimp screwdriver

THE BIRTH OF THE BLUES

A large portion of Swarovski's blue crystal assortment has been in production since the company's early years. Swarovski's initial goal was to produce crystals that imitated the most popular gemstones used in fine jewelry.

The first classic blue shades — aquamarine, light sapphire, sapphire, Montana, and blue zircon — have been manufactured since before 1938. In 1954 Indian sapphire was added and in 1959, Capri blue.

The newer blue shades like indicolite, Pacific opal, Caribbean blue opal, white opal sky blue, and white opal star shine have all been introduced within the last ten years and have been launched based on trend research and market demand.

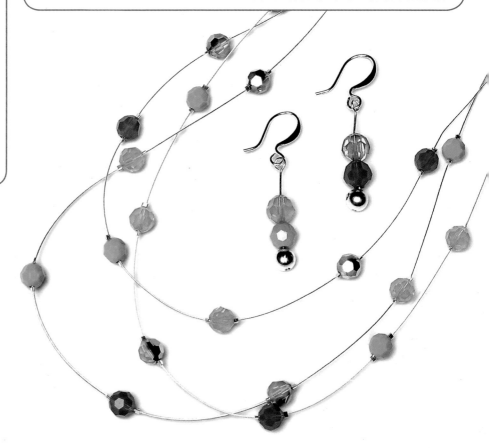

Get your wires in a row

Spacer bars keep memory wire in line

by Jackie Boettcher

Most memory-wire bracelets have one long piece of wire wrapped several times, but I used spacer bars to hold separate pieces of memory wire in place. For a sophisticated cuff, go with a neutral or monochromatic color scheme. Simple crystal earrings extend the sparkle while maintaining the bracelet's subtlety.

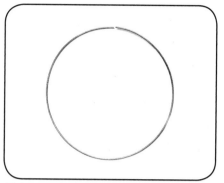

1 bracelet · Using heavy-duty wire cutters, cut a single coil of memory wire. Repeat twice.

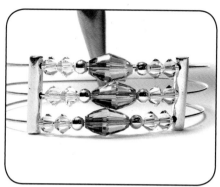

2 Center an oval crystal on each wire. On each end of each wire, string a spacer, two bicone crystals, and the corresponding hole of a spacer bar.

3 On each end, string bicones to within ³⁄₈ in. (1 cm) of the finished length. String the corresponding hole of a spacer bar and make a loop.

4 On a head pin, string a bicone and make a plain loop (Basics, p. 12). Make a total of six bicone units.

5 Open the loop of a bicone unit (Basics) and attach it to one of the bracelet's loops. Close the loop. Repeat with the remaining bicone units.

Supplies

bracelet
- ◆ **3** 9 mm oval crystals
- ◆ **96–126** 4 mm bicone crystals
- ◆ **6** 3 mm round spacers
- ◆ **4** three-hole spacer bars, approximately 15 mm
- ◆ memory wire, bracelet diameter
- ◆ **6** 1-in. (2.5 cm) head pins
- ◆ chainnose and roundnose pliers
- ◆ heavy-duty wire cutters

earrings
- ◆ **2** 9 mm oval crystals
- ◆ **2** 4 mm bicone crystals
- ◆ **2** in. (5 cm) 24-gauge half-hard wire
- ◆ **2** 1-in. (2.5 cm) head pins
- ◆ pair of earring wires
- ◆ chainnose and roundnose pliers
- ◆ diagonal wire cutters

Tips

- • For step 3, string and finish one end of the bracelet at a time. It will be easier to keep the crystals on the wires while you work.
- • When you make the loops on the memory wire, use your sturdiest pair of pliers.
- • Memory wire comes in a variety of bracelet diameters, ranging from 1³⁄₄ in. (4.4 cm) to 2¹⁄₂ in. (6.4 cm). Any variability in the size of your bracelet will come from the wire, so be sure to buy the right size to fit your wrist.

1 **earrings •** On a head pin, string an oval crystal and make a plain loop (Basics, p. 12).

2 Cut a 1-in. (2.5 cm) piece of wire. Make a plain loop on one end. String a bicone crystal and make a plain loop.

3 Open the loops of the bicone unit (Basics). Attach the oval-crystal unit to one end and the loop of an earring wire to the other. Close the loops. Make a second earring to match the first.

Design alternative

For a bracelet-and-earring set that's more fun than formal, use an assortment of crystals. Check stores or online sources for premixed crystals.

Sparkling CZ bracelet

Flash brightly colored
CZs and crystals
in a fun jewelry set

by Monica Lueder

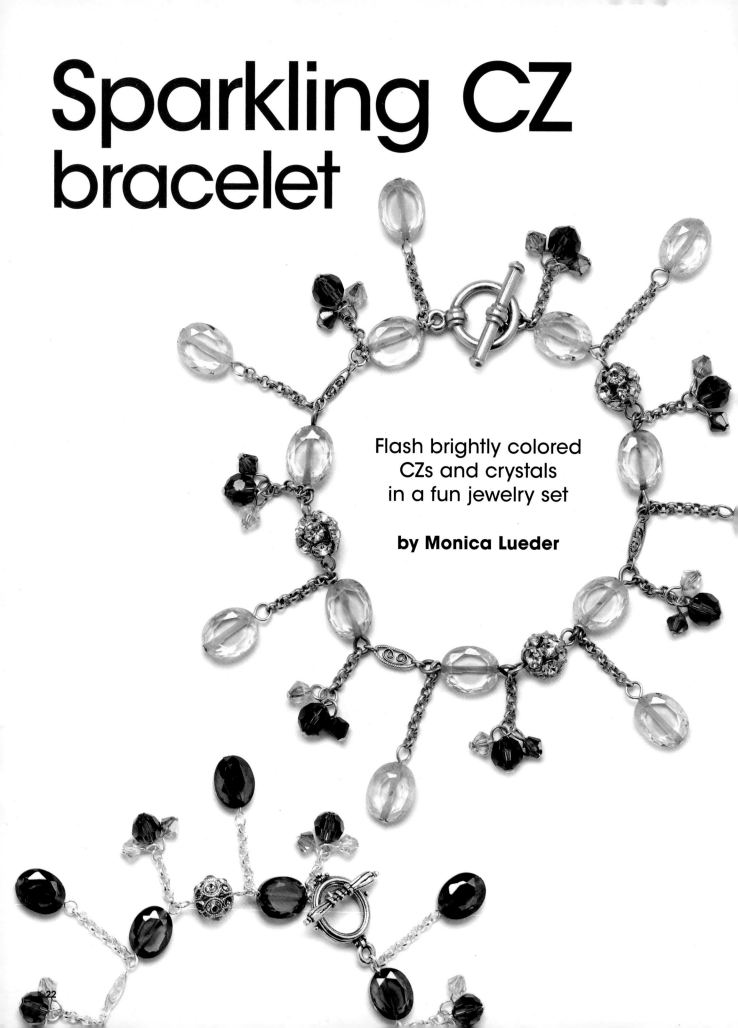

I based my first bracelet — the one with light green, purple, and flashes of orange — on a triad color scheme. A triad is three colors evenly spaced on the color wheel. For my berry-colored bracelet, I used analogous colors, or colors that are adjacent on the color wheel. Whatever color scheme you choose, you'll love the sway and movement of the chain dangles. Earrings with charms and crystals are a decadent addition.

1 bracelet • Cut a 1¼-in. (3.2 cm) piece of wire. Make a plain loop (Basics, p. 12) on one end. String a 10 mm cubic zirconia (CZ) bead and make a plain loop. Make seven to nine CZ units and three or four crystal-studded bead units.

2 Open the loops of a crystal-studded unit (Basics) and attach a CZ unit to each side. Close the loops. On one end, open a 3 mm jump ring (Basics) and attach a filigree link. Close the jump ring. Attach another jump ring and the other side of the link.

Continue attaching CZ units, crystal-studded units, and filigree links until the bracelet is within ½ in. (1.3 cm) of the finished length. End with a CZ unit.

3 On a head pin, string a CZ and make a plain loop. Repeat with a 6 mm bead, a color A bicone crystal, and a color B bicone crystal. Make one of each unit for each two-loop CZ unit in the bracelet.

4 Cut a ⅝-in. (1.6 cm) piece of chain. Open the loop of a one-loop CZ unit and attach the chain. Close the loop. Repeat with the remaining one-loop CZ units.

Cut a ⅜-in. (1 cm) piece of chain. Open the loop of a 6 mm-bead unit and attach a color-A unit, the chain, and a color-B unit. Close the loop. Repeat with the remaining bead and crystal units.

5 On one end, open a loop of the two-loop CZ unit and attach a three-bead dangle. Close the loop. Attach a CZ dangle and the remaining loop of the two-loop CZ unit. Attach the remaining dangles to the two-loop CZ units.

6 On one end, use a 4–5 mm jump ring to attach the toggle half of a clasp. On the other end, open the loop of a two-loop CZ unit and attach the loop half of the clasp.

Supplies

bracelet

- 8-in. (20 cm) strand 10 mm oval cubic zirconia beads
- **3–4** 8 mm crystal-studded beads
- **7–9** 6 mm round beads or crystals
- **14–18** 4 mm bicone crystals, in two colors
- 12–16 in. (31–41 cm) 24-gauge half-hard wire
- 7–9 in. (18–23 cm) rolo chain, 2 mm links
- **3–4** 6–10 mm filigree links
- **21–27** 1-in. (2.5 cm) 24-gauge head pins
- 4–5 mm jump ring
- **6–8** 3 mm jump rings
- toggle clasp
- chainnose and roundnose pliers
- diagonal wire cutters

earrings

- **6** 10–12 mm charms or drops
- **2** 10 mm oval cubic zirconia beads
- **2** 6 mm round beads or crystals
- **20** 4 mm bicone crystals, **6** color A, **6** color B, **6** color C, and **2** color D
- **2** bead caps, with six holes
- 22 in. (56 cm) 24-gauge half-hard wire
- 3 in. (7.6 cm) rolo chain, 2 mm links
- **2** 1-in. (2.5 cm) 24-gauge head pins
- **6** 9–12 mm decorative jump rings
- pair of lever-back earring wires
- chainnose and roundnose pliers
- diagonal wire cutters

1 earrings • On a head pin, string a cubic zirconia (CZ) bead and make a plain loop (Basics, p. 12).

2 Cut a 1-in. (2.5 cm) piece of wire. Make a plain loop on one end. String a bicone crystal and make a plain loop. Make three color-A units, three color-B units, three color-C units, and one color-D unit.

3 Cut a ¾-in. (1.9 cm) piece of chain. Open the loops (Basics) of a color-D unit and attach the chain to one loop and the CZ unit to the other. Close the loops.

4 Cut a ¼-in. (6 mm) piece of chain. Attach one loop of a color-A unit to a charm or drop. Attach the chain to the remaining loop. Attach a color-B unit to the remaining end of the chain. Make three charm dangles.

Tips

- Seven two-loop CZ units will yield a 6¾-in. (17.1 cm) bracelet. Nine CZ units will yield an 8¾-in. (22.2 cm) bracelet. An 8-in. (20 cm) strand of CZs is enough for either size bracelet and a pair of earrings.
- When you make bead units for the earrings, be sure the plain loops are big enough to accommodate the bead cap's holes.

5 Attach a decorative jump ring and a color-C unit. Make three jump-ring dangles.

6 Cut a 1-in. (2.5 cm) piece of wire and make a plain loop on one end. Attach the dangle from step 3. String a 6 mm bead and a bead cap. Make a plain loop.

7 Attach each dangle to a hole of the bead cap, alternating charm dangles and jump-ring dangles.

8 Open the loop of an earring wire. Attach the dangle and close the loop. Make a second earring to match the first.

Design alternative

CZs and crystal-studded beads can be expensive. For a more affordable version, raid your leftover beads and substitute glass or plastic for the most pricey components. You can also simplify the earrings by adding beads to premade chain tassels.

❝I love to work with beautiful gemstones and crystals, and I like adding elegant flair.**❞**

LIGHT UP
chandeliers

Dress up earrings with assorted blue crystals

by Lauren M. Hadley

Go light and bright with shades of aqua and turquoise, or stay serious with slate and Montana blue. With these leaf-themed chandelier findings, you just need to attach a few beads to make a glam accessory.

1 On a decorative head pin, string an 8 mm bead, two spacers, and a 5 mm bicone crystal. Make the first half of a wrapped loop (Basics, p. 12).

2 On a head pin, string a spacer, a rondelle, a spacer, and a 4 mm bicone crystal. Make the first half of a wrapped loop. On a second head pin, string a spacer, a 6 mm crystal, two spacers, and a 4 mm bicone in a second color. Make two of each bead unit.

3 Attach the decorative head pin unit's loop to the center leaf of a chandelier finding. Complete the wraps.

4 Attach the remaining bead units to the respective leaves.

5 Cut a 2-in. (5 cm) piece of wire. Make a plain loop (Basics). String a spacer and a 4 mm bicone. Make a right-angle bend.

6 Curve the wire around a pen barrel.

7 Using chainnose pliers, bend the end of the wire upward. Trim the excess wire and file the end.

8 On a bench block or anvil, gently hammer the earring wire to harden the wire. Flip the earring wire over and hammer the other side.

9 Open the loop of the earring wire (Basics). Attach the dangle and close the loop. Make a second earring to match the first.

Supplies

earrings
- **2** 8 mm beads
- **4** 6 mm faceted rondelles
- **4** 6 mm crystals
- **2** 5 mm bicone crystals
- **10** 4 mm bicone crystals, **6** in one color and **4** in another
- **26** 3–4 mm flat spacers
- pair of 32 mm leaf-themed chandelier findings (beadsgalorestore.etsy.com)
- 4 in. (10 cm) 20-gauge half-hard wire
- **2** 2-in. (5 cm) decorative head pins
- **8** 1½-in. (3.8 cm) head pins
- chainnose and roundnose pliers
- diagonal wire cutters
- bench block or anvil
- hammer
- metal file or emery board

Tip

Try mixing opaque and transparent beads. The overall effect will be beautiful, as long as you keep the colors within the same family.

Display a cluster of
crystals

by Mary Bloomsburg

Top-drilled crystals sparkle in a necklace, bracelet, and earrings

Show off a vibrant spectrum of colors in this easy jewelry set. A few top-drilled crystals on a single wire become a quick pendant, and clustering crystals make a striking focus of the accompanying bracelet. For a small dose of color, attach a single crystal to an earring wire. You'll have the whole set done in under an hour.

Crystal colors

In the orange jewelry, I used Swarovski crystals in:
- hyacinth (color A)
- topaz (color B)
- olivine (color C)

In the purple jewelry:
- tanzanite (color A)
- violet (color B)
- burgundy (color C)

1 necklace • Cut a piece of beading wire (Basics, p. 12). On the wire, center an alternating pattern of three 8 mm color A bicone crystals and three 8 mm color B bicones. Over both ends, string a 6 mm color C bicone and a 4 mm color B bicone.

2 On each end, string: 4 mm color C bicone, 6 mm color A bicone, 6 mm color B bicone, 6 mm color C bicone, 8 mm color A bicone, 8 mm color B bicone, 6 mm color C bicone, 8 mm color A bicone, 8 mm color B bicone.

3 On each end, string an alternating pattern of three 6 mm color C bicones and three 3 mm spacers. String a curved tube bead and a spacer. Repeat until the strand is within 1 in. (2.5 cm) of the finished length, ending with a curved tube.

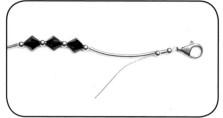

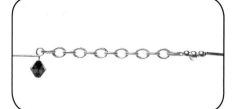

4 On one end, string a spacer, a crimp bead, a spacer, and a lobster claw clasp. Repeat on the other end, substituting a 2-in. (5 cm) piece of chain for the clasp. Check the fit, and add or remove beads from each end if necessary. Go back through the beads just strung and tighten the wire. Crimp the crimp beads (Basics) and trim the excess wire. Use chainnose pliers to close a crimp cover over each crimp bead.

5 On a head pin, string a 6 mm color C bicone. Make the first half of a wrapped loop (Basics). Attach the loop to the end of the chain and complete the wraps.

1 bracelet • Cut a piece of beading wire (Basics, p. 12). On the wire, string a 6 mm color C bicone crystal, an 8 mm color A bicone, and an 8 mm color B bicone. Repeat five times, then string a 6 mm color C bicone. Center the beads.

2 On each end, string a 4–5 mm spacer and a curved tube bead. Check the fit, allowing 1 in. (2.5 cm) for finishing. If you need to shorten the bracelet, remove pairs of color A and color B bicones. If you need to lengthen the bracelet, string more 3 mm spacers on the end.

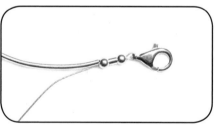

3 Finish as in steps 4 and 5 of the necklace, using a 1-in. (2.5 cm) piece of chain for the extender.

earrings • Open a jump ring (Basics, p. 12). Attach an 8 mm bicone crystal and the loop of an earring wire. Close the jump ring. Make a second earring to match the first.

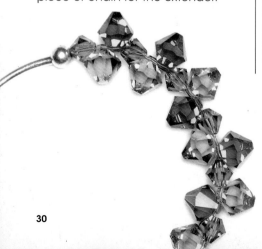

Supplies

necklace (purple 18 in./46 cm; orange 19 in./48 cm)
- **6-8** 26–30 mm curved tube beads
- **14** 8 mm bicone crystals, top drilled, **7** color A, **7** color B
- **4** 6 mm bicone crystals, top drilled, **2** color A, **2** color B
- **24-30** 6 mm bicone crystals, color C
- **3** 4 mm bicone crystals, **1** color B, **2** color C
- **26-34** 3 mm round spacers
- flexible beading wire, .014 or .015
- 1½-in. (3.8cm) head pin
- **2** crimp beads
- **2** crimp covers
- lobster claw clasp
- 2 in. (5 cm) chain for extender, 4–5 mm links
- chainnose and roundnose pliers
- diagonal wire cutters
- crimping pliers (optional)

bracelet
- **2** 26–30 mm curved tube beads
- **12** 8 mm bicone crystals, top drilled, **6** color A, **6** color B
- **8** 6 mm bicone crystals, color C
- **2** 4–5 mm round spacers
- **4-8** 3 mm round spacers
- flexible beading wire, .014 or .015
- 1½-in. (3.8cm) head pin
- **2** crimp beads
- **2** crimp covers
- lobster claw clasp
- 1 in. (2.5 cm) chain for extender, 4–5 mm links
- chainnose and roundnose pliers
- diagonal wire cutters
- crimping pliers (optional)

earrings
- **2** 8 mm bicone crystals, top drilled
- **2** 5–6 mm jump rings
- pair of earring wires
- chainnose and roundnose pliers

Extended
style

by Angie D'Amato

One long strand glimmers without end

This inexpensive necklace is a snap to string. The metallic finish on the fire-polished crystals glams up this long look. Wear the necklace as one long strand, or loop it around your neck for multistrand magic. Or try a hinged twister clasp to convert this continuous loop into a shorter necklace. Ease a few stretchy strands onto your wrist as glitzy companions.

1 necklace • Cut a piece of beading wire (Basics, p. 12). String crystals until the strand is within 1 in. (2.5 cm) of the finished length.

2 On one end, string a crimp bead, a crystal, and a crimp bead.

3 String the other end through the last few beads strung. Check the fit, and add or remove beads if necessary. Tighten the wire and crimp the crimp beads (Basics). Trim the excess wire.

Tips

• For speedy stringing, thread the beading wire through the 8 mm beads while they're still on their original string. When you've strung enough beads on the beading wire, pull out the original string.
• To make sure the necklace loops around multiple times, avoid overtightening the wire in step 3.

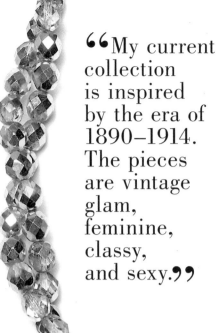

My current collection is inspired by the era of 1890–1914. The pieces are vintage glam, feminine, classy, and sexy.

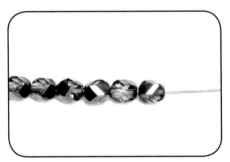

1 bracelet • Decide how long you want your bracelet to be, add 3 in. (7.6 cm), and cut a piece of ribbon elastic to that length. String beads until the bracelet is the finished length.

2 Tie a surgeon's knot (Basics, p. 12). Trim the ends and glue the knot.

Supplies

necklace 64 in. (1.6 m)
- ◆ **4** 16-in. (41 cm) strands 8 mm Czech fire-polished crystals
- ◆ flexible beading wire, .018 or .019
- ◆ **2** crimp beads
- ◆ crimping pliers
- ◆ diagonal wire cutters

bracelet
- ◆ **18-24** 8 mm glass beads per bracelet
- ◆ ribbon elastic
- ◆ G-S Hypo Cement

Design alternative

To add more dimension to your necklace, combine two or more shapes of Czech glass beads.

Twinkling, light, and airy

Crimp your style with sparkling possibilities

by Mia Gofar

This ethereal look comes from a lot of down-to-earth crimping. Everything about the necklace-bracelet-earring set can be altered to fit your style. Change the size of the crystals or the length of the beading wire pieces. Or vary the elements in each piece of jewelry.

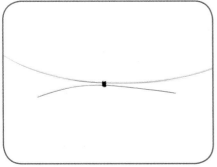

1a necklace • Cut a piece of beading wire (Basics, p. 12). Center a crimp bead.

    b Cut a 2-in. (5 cm) piece of beading wire. String it through the crimp bead so the bead is centered on the short wire. Flatten the crimp bead (Basics).

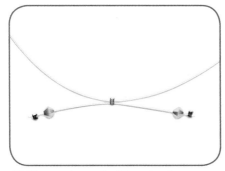

2 On each end of the short wire, string a bicone crystal and a crimp bead. Flatten the crimp beads.

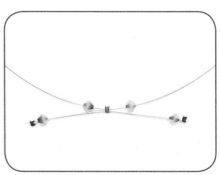

3 On each end of the long wire, string a bicone.

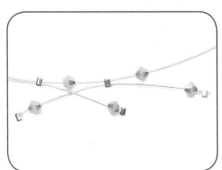

4 On each end of the long wire, string a crimp bead about ½ in. (1.3 cm) from the last crimp bead strung. Follow steps 1b, 2, and 3. Repeat until the short-wire segments reach the finished length. Check the fit. Allowing 1 in. (2.5 cm) for the finishing, trim the long wire to the finished length.

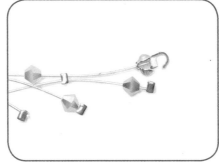

5 On each end of the long wire, string a bead tip and a crimp bead. Flatten the crimp bead. Use chainnose pliers to close the bead tip over the crimp.

6 On one end, string a lobster claw clasp on the loop of the bead tip. Use chainnose pliers to close the loop. Repeat on the other end, substituting a split ring for the clasp.

Supplies

necklace 18 in. (46 cm)
- **80-92** 4 mm bicone crystals
- flexible beading wire, .018 or .019
- 6 mm split ring
- **2** bead tips, clamshell style
- **80-92** crimp beads
- lobster claw clasp
- chainnose pliers
- diagonal wire cutters

bracelet
- **26-30** 4 mm bicone crystals
- flexible beading wire, .018 or .019
- **2** bead tips, clamshell style
- **26-30** crimp beads
- magnetic clasp
- chainnose pliers
- diagonal wire cutters

earrings
- **10** 4 mm bicone crystals
- flexible beading wire, .018 or .019
- **2** 2-in. (5 cm) head pins
- **12** crimp beads
- pair of earring wires
- chainnose and roundnose pliers
- diagonal wire cutters

Tips

- Because the beading wire is exposed, I used .018 24k-plated gold beading wire and .019 sterling silver. For a stiffer bracelet, use heavier (.024) beading wire.
- I strung Swarovski olivine crystals on the gold necklace and white alabaster AB2X on the silver.
- To save time, cut all of the short pieces of wire first. For the necklace, you'll need 27 to 35 short pieces; for the bracelet, cut 13 to 15.

bracelet • Follow the necklace instructions, but cut the short wires ¾ in. (1.9 cm) long, space the crimp beads ¼ in. (6 mm) apart on the longer wire, and substitute a magnetic clasp for the lobster claw clasp and split ring.

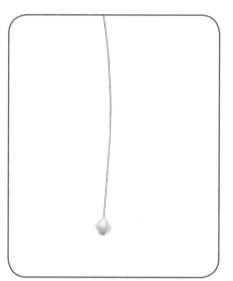

1 **earrings** • On a head pin, string a bicone crystal.

2a On the head pin, string a crimp bead ½ in. (1.3 cm) from the bicone.

b Cut a ½-in. (1.3 cm) piece of beading wire. String it through the crimp bead so the bead is centered on the short wire. Flatten the crimp bead (Basics, p. 12). Follow necklace step 2.

3 On the head pin, string a crimp bead ½ in. (1.3 cm) from the last crimp bead strung. Repeat earring step 2b.

"I bead anywhere and whenever possible."

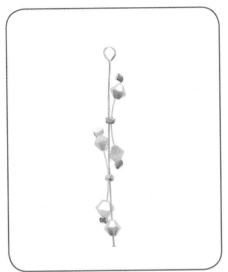

4 Make a plain loop (Basics).

5 Open the loop of an earring wire (Basics). Attach the dangle and close the loop. Make a second earring to match the first.

Design alternative

For a bolder look, try this design with small briolettes. Black beading wire picks up the details in rutilated quartz.

Flurry
of blue

Meet the season in snowflake earrings

by Jenna Colyar-Cooper

Welcome the snowfall with a pair of snowflake earrings boasting three tiers of sparkling crystals. If you prefer a lighter dusting, attach one crystal to each loop of the chandelier component.

1 On a head pin, string a 6 mm crystal. Make a wrapped loop (Basics, p. 12). Make three 6 mm units.

2 Cut a 2-in. (5 cm) piece of wire. Make the first half of a wrapped loop on one end. Attach a 6 mm unit and complete the wraps. Repeat with the remaining 6 mm units.

3 On each wire, string a 4–5 mm crystal and make a wrapped loop.

4 Cut a 2-in. (5 cm) piece of wire. Make the first half of a wrapped loop on one end. Attach a dangle and complete the wraps. String a 4 mm crystal and make the first half of a wrapped loop. Repeat with the remaining dangles.

5 Attach each dangle to a loop of a snowflake component and complete the wraps.

6 Open the loop of an earring wire (Basics). Attach the top loop of the snowflake component and close the loop. Make a second earring to match the first.

Supplies

Snowflake components from Fusion Beads, fusionbeads.com.

- ◆ **2** 25 mm snowflake chandelier components
- ◆ **6** 6 mm crystals
- ◆ **6** 4–5 mm crystals
- ◆ **6** 4 mm crystals
- ◆ 2 ft. (61 cm) 24-gauge half-hard wire
- ◆ **6** 1½-in. (3.8 cm) head pins
- ◆ pair of earring wires
- ◆ chainnose and roundnose pliers
- ◆ diagonal wire cutters

Design alternative

Change the position of your earrings by adding a jump ring to the component's top loop. This subtle change will make the snowflake visible from the side.

It's all in
the details

String a bouquet of color in this quick set

Tiny details, such as rosebud beads and flower-shaped bead caps, give a simple design panache. The effect is subtle, but it packs more punch than plain round beads and bead caps.

by Karen Burdette

1 necklace · Cut a piece of beading wire (Basics, p. 12). Center a rosebud bead, a bicone crystal, and a bead.

2 On each end, string: bead cap, bead, bead cap, bead, bicone, bead. Repeat until the strand is within 1 in. (2.5 cm) of the finished length.

Supplies

necklace 16 in. (41 cm)
- ◆ **2** 8-in. (20 cm) strands 7–9 mm rosebud beads
- ◆ **13–17** 4 mm bicone crystals
- ◆ **24–32** 6–8 mm flower-shaped bead caps or spacer beads
- ◆ flexible beading wire, .014 or .015
- ◆ **2** crimp beads
- ◆ lobster claw clasp and soldered jump ring
- ◆ chainnose or crimping pliers
- ◆ diagonal wire cutters

earrings
- ◆ **4** 7–9 mm rosebud beads
- ◆ **2** 4 mm bicone crystals
- ◆ **2** 6–8 mm flower-shaped bead caps or spacer beads
- ◆ **2** 1½-in. (3.8 cm) head pins
- ◆ pair of lever-back earring wires
- ◆ chainnose and roundnose pliers
- ◆ diagonal wire cutters

3 On one end, string a crimp bead, a bicone, and a lobster claw clasp. Repeat on the other end, substituting a soldered jump ring for the clasp. Check the fit, and add or remove beads if necessary. Go back through the last few beads strung and tighten the wire. Crimp the crimp beads (Basics) and trim the excess wire.

1 **earrings** · On a head pin, string a bicone crystal, a rosebud bead, a bead cap, and a bead. Make a plain loop (Basics, p. 12).

2 Open the loop of an earring wire (Basics). Attach the dangle and close the loop. Make a second earring to match the first.

Tip

Rosebud beads and flower-shaped bead caps are available in a variety of colors. If you're feeling adventurous, mix and match them to produce creative combinations.

Cosmic RINGS bracelet

Use uncommon crystals in a distinctive bracelet-and-earrings set

by Karla Schafer

Two crystal cosmic rings stacked together make a prominent focal piece for an easy bracelet. The faceted rings create a fancy contrast to casual leather cord. Add a quick pair of earrings for a just-right balance of edgy and elegant.

1 bracelet • Cut a 10-in. (25 cm) piece of leather cord. Center two cosmic rings. Over both ends, string two or three soldered jump rings or decorative beads.

2 With both ends, tie an overhand knot (Basics, p. 12) next to the rings or beads. Repeat steps 1 and 2.

> **"I used cosmic rings in crystal golden shadow (left) and crystal CAL V SI (right).99**

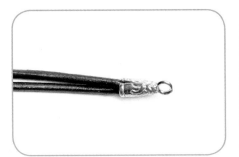

3 On each side, trim the ends to within 1 in. (2.5 cm) of the finished length and apply glue. Place the ends in a crimp end and use chainnose pliers to gently squeeze the crimp end.

4 Open a jump ring (Basics) and attach a loop of a crimp end and a lobster claw clasp. Close the jump ring. Repeat on the other end, substituting a soldered jump ring or decorative ring for the clasp.

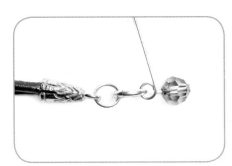

5 On a head pin, string a crystal. Make the first half of a wrapped loop (Basics). Attach the soldered jump ring or decorative ring and complete the wraps.

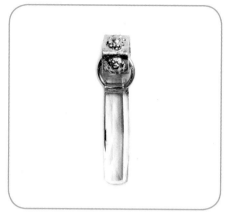

1 earrings • Open a jump ring (Basics, p. 12) and attach a pendant and a soldered jump ring or decorative bead. Close the jump ring.

2 Use a jump ring to attach the soldered jump ring or decorative bead and an earring wire. Make a second earring to match the first.

Tips

• Select the 30 mm crystal cosmic rings first, since there are fewer colors available in this size than in smaller sizes.

• Before placing the leather ends in a crimp end, make sure to trim both leather ends evenly.

"Though I do not consider myself a girly girl, I do like my bling.**"**

Design alternative

Feeling square? In this version, I used square cosmic rings, square decorative rings, and a square crystal for the dangle. I substituted four 1 mm pieces of leather cord for the two 2 mm pieces.

Supplies

bracelet
- ◆ 30 mm crystal cosmic ring
- ◆ 20 mm crystal cosmic ring
- ◆ 6 mm crystal
- ◆ 16–20 in. (41–51 cm) round leather cord, 2 mm diameter
- ◆ 1½-in. (3.8 cm) head pin
- ◆ **2** 5 mm jump rings
- ◆ **5–7** 7 mm soldered jump rings or decorative beads
- ◆ **2** crimp ends, 3 mm opening
- ◆ lobster claw clasp and soldered jump ring
- ◆ chainnose and roundnose pliers
- ◆ diagonal wire cutters
- ◆ G-S Hypo Cement

earrings
- ◆ **2** 20 mm crystal column pendants
- ◆ **4** 7 mm jump rings
- ◆ **2** 7 mm soldered jump rings or decorative beads
- ◆ pair of earring wires
- ◆ chainnose and roundnose pliers, or **2** pairs of chainnose pliers
- ◆ diagonal wire cutters

Knockout earrings

Barbell-shaped crystals give earrings some fashion muscle

by Jenna Colyar-Cooper

For a pair of fabulous earrings, barbell-shaped crystals and jump rings make a winning combination. Pick contrasting crystal colors for a high-impact design. In 15 minutes, you'll have modern earrings that pack a style punch.

1 Open a jump ring (Basics, p. 12). String a color A barbell-shaped crystal and close the jump ring.

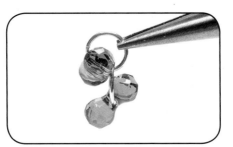

2 Open another jump ring. String a color B barbell and attach the previous jump ring. Close the jump ring. Use jump rings to attach a color A, color B, and color A barbell.

3 Open the loop of an earring wire (Basics). Attach the dangle and close the loop. Make a second earring to match the first.

Supplies

- **10** 11 mm barbell-shaped crystals, **6** in color A, **4** in color B
- **10** 7.3 mm jump rings
- pair of earring wires
- chainnose and roundnose pliers, or **2** pairs of chainnose pliers

Design alternative

For party-worthy baubles, try long earrings with a single color. For each earring, I used 12 crystal-colored barbells.

Gemstones

Balanced drape

Chandelier components give a necklace and bracelet a flexible design

by Lauren M. Hadley

To make a shimmering necklace that drapes gracefully, start with decorative chandelier components, then pick chain and gemstones that work with the components' style. I like pale, ethereal labradorite or pink Peruvian opal as options. In the bracelet, using only two gemstones will keep the focus on the ornate components.

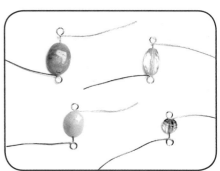

1 necklace • Cut a 3-in. (7.6 cm) piece of wire. Make the first half of a wrapped loop (Basics, p. 12). String a 13–16 mm (large) bead and make the first half of a wrapped loop. Make three large-bead units. Make two 10–12 mm (medium) bead units, 14 8–9 mm (small) bead units, and six round-bead units.

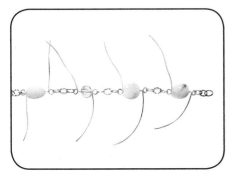

2 To make the first (longest) strand: Cut nine ½-in. (1.3 cm) pieces of 3–4 mm (small) cable chain. Center a piece of chain. On each end, attach: small-bead unit, chain, round-bead unit, chain, small-bead unit, chain, small-bead unit, chain. Complete the wraps as you go.

To make the fifth (shortest) strand: Cut seven ½-in. (1.3 cm) pieces of small chain. Attach bead units as in the first strand, omitting the chain on each end. Leave the end loops unwrapped.

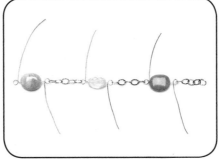

3 To make the third strand: Cut six ¾-in. (1.9 cm) pieces of small chain. Center a large-bead unit. On each end, attach: chain, medium-bead unit, chain, large-bead unit, chain. Complete the wraps as you go.

To make the second and fourth strands: Cut two pieces of small chain (mine are 8 and 7½ in./20 and 19.1 cm).

4 Open a jump ring (Basics). Attach one end of the first strand and an end loop of a five-to-one component. Close the jump ring. Repeat on the other end. Use jump rings to attach the second, third, and fourth strands and the corresponding loops of the component. Connect the open wraps on each end of the fifth strand with the corresponding loops of the component. Complete the wraps.

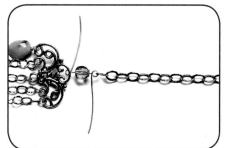

5 Decide how long you want your necklace to be, subtract the length of the beaded section, and cut a piece of 5–6 mm (large) cable chain to that length. Cut the chain in half. Use a round-bead unit to attach the remaining loop of one component and a chain. Complete the wraps. Repeat on the other side.

6 Check the fit, allowing 1 in. (2.5 cm) for finishing, and trim chain from each end if necessary. On each end, use a small-bead unit to attach half of a clasp.

Tips

• For an economical alternative, use a graduated strand of 8–16 mm beads.
• Try jasper or another gemstone that shows a range of colors.

66My favorite gemstone is rough-cut labradorite because it reminds me of brilliant lightning flashing across a dark, ominous grey sky.**99**

Supplies

necklace (labradorite 20 in./ 51 cm; pink opal 21½ in./54.6 cm)
- ◆ **3** 13–16 mm beads
- ◆ **2** 10–12 mm beads
- ◆ **14** 8–9 mm beads
- ◆ **6** 6 mm round beads
- ◆ 75 in. (1.9 m) 24-gauge half-hard wire
- ◆ 8–12 in. (20–30 cm) cable chain, 5–6 mm links
- ◆ 30–35 in. (76–89 cm) cable chain, 3–4 mm links
- ◆ **2** five-to-one chandelier components
- ◆ **8–10** 4 mm jump rings
- ◆ toggle clasp
- ◆ chainnose and roundnose pliers
- ◆ diagonal wire cutters

bracelet
- ◆ **2** 8–9 mm beads
- ◆ 6 in. (15 cm) 24-gauge half-hard wire
- ◆ 10–12 in. (25–30 cm) cable chain, 5–6 mm links
- ◆ **2** five-to-one chandelier components
- ◆ **12** 4 mm jump rings
- ◆ toggle clasp
- ◆ chainnose and roundnose pliers
- ◆ diagonal wire cutters

1 bracelet • Cut five 1¼–1¾ (3.2–4.4 cm) pieces of chain. Open a jump ring (Basics, p. 12). Attach a chain and a loop of a five-to-one component and close the jump ring. Use a jump ring to attach each end of each chain and the corresponding loop of the component.

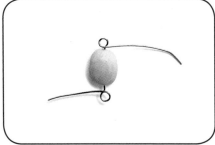

2 Cut a 3-in. (7.6 cm) piece of wire. Make the first half of a wrapped loop (Basics). String an 8–9 mm bead and make the first half of a wrapped loop. Make two bead units.

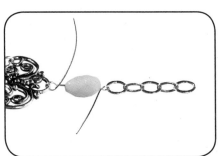

3 Cut two 1–1½-in. (2.5–3.8 cm) pieces of chain. Attach one loop of a bead unit to the remaining loop of a five-to-one component and the other loop to a chain. Complete the wraps. Repeat on the other end with the remaining bead unit and the remaining piece of chain.

4 Check the fit, allowing 1 in. (2.5 cm) for finishing. Trim chain if necessary. On each end, use a jump ring to attach half of a clasp and the chain.

Design alternative

Make earrings using three-to-one (instead of five-to-one) components. The smaller scale won't overpower the necklace and bracelet.

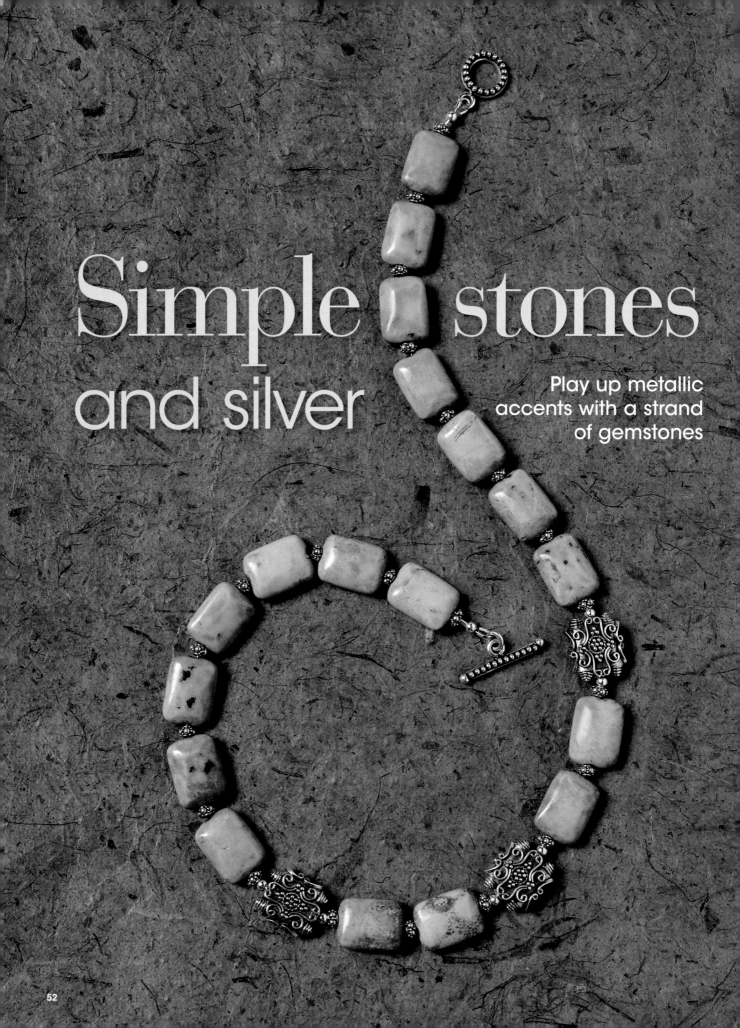

Simple stones
and silver

Play up metallic
accents with a strand
of gemstones

by Rupa Balachandar

For a quick necklace, strategically string silver accent beads flanked by rectangular gemstones. Smooth stones are a soothing contrast to the ornate scrollwork of the silver beads. Complete the ensemble with a pair of easy earrings.

1 necklace • Cut a piece of beading wire (Basics, p. 12). String a round spacer, an accent bead, and a round spacer. Center the beads.

2 On each end, string: flat spacer, rectangular bead, flat spacer, rectangle, flat spacer, round spacer, accent bead, round spacer.

3 String an alternating pattern of flat spacers and rectangles until the strand is within 1 in. (2.5 cm) of the finished length. End with a flat spacer.

4 On each end, string a crimp bead, a round spacer, a Wire Guardian, and half of a clasp. Check the fit, and add or remove beads if necessary. Go back through the last few beads strung and tighten the wire. Crimp the crimp bead (Basics) and trim the excess wire.

Supplies

Supplies available from Rupa B. Designs, rupab.com.

necklace 18½ in. (47 cm)
- 16-in. (41 cm) strand 18 mm rectangular beads
- **3** 17 mm square accent beads
- **18–26** 4 mm flat spacers
- **8** 3 mm round spacers
- flexible beading wire, .014 or .015
- **2** crimp beads
- **2** Wire Guardians
- toggle clasp
- chainnose or crimping pliers
- diagonal wire cutters

earrings
- **2** 18 mm rectangular beads
- **2** 4 mm flat spacers
- **4** 3 mm round spacers
- **2** 2½-in. (6.4 cm) decorative head pins
- pair of lever-back earring wires
- chainnose and roundnose pliers
- diagonal wire cutters

Tips

- Use accent beads that mimic the shape of the gemstones.
- Choose a detailed toggle clasp to complement the design on the accent beads.

1 **earrings** • On a decorative head pin, string a round spacer, a flat spacer, a rectangular bead, and a round spacer. Make a wrapped loop (Basics, p. 12).

2 Open the loop of an earring wire (Basics). Attach the dangle and close the loop. Make a second earring to match the first.

"I can't help but think that my jewelry tells stories of my passions, emotions, and values — it defines my personality.**"**

Design alternative

For a necklace with a pendant, make one bead unit with a spacer, an accent bead, and a spacer. Make a second bead unit, substituting a rectangular bead for the accent bead. Attach the two bead units and center the pendant on the wire.

Fast
fall fashion

A necklace comes together
quickly with elaborate chain

by DonnaMarie Bates

This ingenious cable chain has large oval links attached, so to make an abundantly detailed necklace, you simply add beads. Try warm orange shades of carnelian, or cool things down with blue chalcedony or green jasper. With just a few wrapped loops, you'll be on the fast track to seasonal style.

1 necklace • To make a briolette unit: Cut a 3-in. (7.6 cm) piece of wire. String a briolette and make a set of wraps above it (Basics, p. 12). String a 5 mm bead and a pearl or a bicone crystal, and make the first half of a wrapped loop (Basics) perpendicular to the briolette. Make six briolette units. Set aside one unit for step 6.

2 To make a bead unit: On a head pin, string three or four 8–12 mm beads, 5 mm beads, bicones, or pearls. Make the first half of a wrapped loop. Make four pairs of bead units.

3 Decide how long you want your necklace to be and cut a piece of chain to that length. Make sure the center link is a 9 mm link without an attached 20 mm link. Attach a briolette unit to the center link and complete the wraps.

4 On each side, attach a bead unit to the next 9 mm link without an attached 20 mm link. Complete the wraps. Repeat five times, using the remaining briolette and bead units.

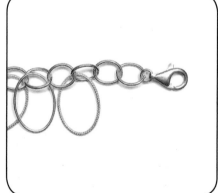

5 Check the fit and trim chain from each end if necessary. Open a jump ring (Basics). On one end, attach a lobster claw clasp and close the jump ring. Repeat on the other end, substituting a soldered jump ring for the clasp.

6 Attach a briolette unit to the soldered jump ring. Complete the wraps.

Supplies

necklace 16 in. (41 cm)

- ◆ **6** 10–17 mm briolettes, in two styles
- ◆ **16–20** 8–12 mm beads
- ◆ **8–12** 5 mm round beads
- ◆ **11–15** 4 mm bicone crystals
- ◆ **3–7** 3–4 mm pearls
- ◆ 18 in. (46 cm) 24- or 26-gauge half-hard wire
- ◆ 16–19 in. (41–48 cm) chain, 9 mm and 20 mm links (Silver in Style, silverinstylellc.com)
- ◆ **8** 2½-in. (6.4 cm) head pins
- ◆ **2** 4 mm jump rings
- ◆ lobster claw clasp and soldered jump ring
- ◆ chainnose and roundnose pliers
- ◆ diagonal wire cutters

earrings

- ◆ **2** 10–17 mm briolettes
- ◆ **2** 4 mm bicone crystals
- ◆ 6 in. (15 cm) 24- or 26-gauge half-hard wire
- ◆ **2** 4–6 mm decorative jump rings
- ◆ pair of earring wires
- ◆ chainnose and roundnose pliers
- ◆ diagonal wire cutters

Tip

Because this chain has additional links, it costs more than most sterling silver chain. It's sold by the foot, so consider making a bracelet too. You can make a 17-in. (43 cm) necklace and a 7-in. (18 cm) bracelet from 2 ft. (61 cm) of chain.

1 earrings • Cut a 3-in. (7.6 cm) piece of wire. String a briolette and make a set of wraps above it (Basics, p. 12). String a bicone crystal and make the first half of a wrapped loop (Basics) perpendicular to the briolette.

2 Attach the loop to a decorative jump ring. Complete the wraps. Open the loop of an earring wire (Basics). Attach the dangle and close the loop. Make a second earring to match the first.

Tied to turquoise

Whip up a necklace and earrings with turquoise and knotted cord

by Irina Miech

With so many cord colors and varieties of turquoise, it's easy to choose a combination that you feel attached to. Try bright blue turquoise and matching cord for sweet femininity. Or pair green gems and black cord for earthy sophistication. Sans clasp, this lengthy necklace slips easily over your head. Simple nugget earrings set your look in stone.

1 necklace • Tie an overhand knot (Basics, p. 12) 4 in. (10 cm) from the end of a beading cord. String: 4 mm spacer, 6 mm round bead, 9 mm spacer, round, 4 mm spacer. Tie an overhand knot.

2 Tie an overhand knot 1 in. (2.5 cm) from the previous knot. String three to five gemstone chips and tie an overhand knot.

3 Tie an overhand knot 1 in. (2.5 cm) from the previous knot. String a 4 mm spacer, a nugget, and a 4 mm spacer. Tie an overhand knot.

4 Repeat the patterns in steps 1–3 (or string new patterns) until the necklace is within 4 in. (10 cm) of the finished length.

5 On one end, tie an overhand knot 1 in. (2.5 cm) from the previous knot. String a nugget. On the other end, tie an overhand knot 1 in. (2.5 cm) from the previous knot and string a few nuggets. Tie the two ends together with a surgeon's knot (Basics). Trim the ends and glue the knot.

Tip

To tie a knot close to a bead: Use roundnose pliers to grasp the cord next to the bead, then tie a knot by looping the cord around the pliers' tip. As you tighten the knot, slide the pliers out.

1 earrings • On a head pin, string a spacer, a nugget, and a spacer. Make a wrapped loop (Basics, p. 12).

2 Open the loop of an earring wire (Basics) and attach the dangle. Close the loop. Make a second earring to match the first.

Design alternative

Instead of tying knots, string bead bumpers. Then move beads along the beading cord.

Supplies

necklace (green 18 in./46 cm)
- ◆ **4-6** 18–22 mm nuggets
- ◆ 16-in. (41 cm) strand 8–12 mm gemstone chips
- ◆ **12-16** 6 mm round beads
- ◆ **7-9** 9 mm spacers in two styles
- ◆ **16-20** 4 mm spacers
- ◆ card of silk beading cord, size 4
- ◆ roundnose pliers
- ◆ diagonal wire cutters or scissors
- ◆ G-S Hypo Cement

earrings
- ◆ **2** 18–22 mm nuggets
- ◆ **4** 4 mm spacers
- ◆ **2** 2-in. (5 cm) head pins
- ◆ pair of lever-back earring wires
- ◆ chainnose and roundnose pliers
- ◆ diagonal wire cutters

> 66Working with turquoise always makes me think of Santa Fe and the timeless beauty of its landscape and people.99

Raising the
style bar

by Sue Godfrey

Make a lush bracelet with bar-shaped components

You'll love these ingenious bar-shaped caterpillar components. They have lots of loops, giving you multiple design options. I chose to attach a variety of beads — smooth and faceted, opaque and transparent, round and flat. After making so many wrapped loops, I opted for the simplest bead-and-chain earrings, but you could also make cluster earrings to carry on the theme.

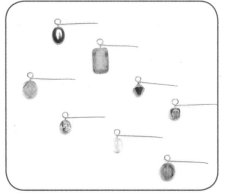

1 **bracelet** • On a head pin, string a 5–12 mm bead. Make the first half of a wrapped loop (Basics, p. 12). Make 60 bead units.

2 Attach a bead unit to a loop of a caterpillar component. Complete the wraps. Attach four bead units to each loop, completing the wraps as you go. Make three beaded components.

3 Decide how long you want your bracelet to be and cut two pieces of beading wire (Basics). On each wire, center the corresponding holes of a beaded component.

4 On each side, over both wires, string a 4 mm bicone crystal, a metal bead, and a 4 mm bicone. On each wire, string the corresponding holes of a beaded component.

5 On each side, over both wires, string: 5–6 mm bicone crystal, metal bead, 5–6 mm bicone, spacer, crimp bead, spacer, half of a clasp. Check the fit, and add or remove beads from each end if necessary. Go back through the beads just strung and tighten the wires. Crimp the crimp bead (Basics) and trim the excess wire.

❝I like to use glass that resembles stone and mix it with other elements like pearls and crystals.❞

Supplies

bracelet
- ◆ **60** 5–12 mm beads
- ◆ **4** 7–12 mm metal accent beads
- ◆ **4–6** 5–6 mm bicone crystals
- ◆ **4–8** 4 mm bicone crystals
- ◆ **4** 4–5 mm spacers
- ◆ **3** 21 mm caterpillar components with five loops (Midwest Beads, midwestbeads.com)
- ◆ flexible beading wire, .014 or .015
- ◆ **60** 1½-in. (3.8 cm) head pins
- ◆ **2** crimp beads
- ◆ toggle clasp
- ◆ chainnose and roundnose pliers
- ◆ diagonal wire cutters
- ◆ crimping pliers (optional)

earrings
- ◆ **2** 5–12 mm beads
- ◆ **1** in. (2.5 cm) chain, 4–5 mm links
- ◆ **2** 1½-in. (3.8 cm) head pins
- ◆ pair of earring wires
- ◆ chainnose and roundnose pliers
- ◆ diagonal wire cutters

Design alternative

To make a bracelet with fewer bead units, try caterpillar components with three loops rather than five. Omit the 5 mm beads and use more 8–12 mm beads. You'll only need a total of 36 bead units.

1 earrings · On a head pin, string a bead. Make the first half of a wrapped loop (Basics, p. 12).

2 Cut a piece of chain with two links. Attach the bead unit and complete the wraps.

3 Open the loop of an earring wire (Basics). Attach the dangle and close the loop. Make a second earring to match the first.

Tips

• To save time in designing, first make three of each type of bead unit — for example, make three grey pearl units, three purple rectangle units, etc., until you've made three each with 20 kinds of beads. Then, attach each type of unit to the corresponding loop of each component and complete the wraps.

• Choose metal accent beads based on how long you want the bracelet to be. I used 7 mm metal beads in the brown (6¾-in./17.1 cm) bracelet and 12 mm beads in the lavender (7¾-in./19.7 cm) bracelet.

• You can also vary the size and quantity of crystals or spacers to alter the length.

Drop everything for this
swingy bracelet

Dangling drops sparkle in a bevy of shapes and colors

by Sarah Caligiuri

Can only beads of a feather hang together? Of course not. Mixing the many shapes available in top-drilled gems and beads and using an expressive color palette can make a simple design extraordinary. A little wire wrapping adds some extra sheen to the bracelet and mismatched earrings.

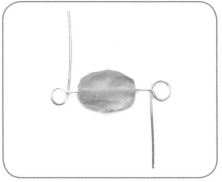

1 **bracelet** • Cut a 3-in. (7.6 cm) piece of wire. On one end, make the first half of a wrapped loop (Basics, p. 12). String an 8 mm oval bead and make the first half of a wrapped loop.

2 Decide how long you want your bracelet to be. Subtract the length of the bead unit and a lobster claw clasp and cut a piece of cable chain to that length. Attach one end of the chain to one of the bead unit's loops. Attach the lobster claw clasp to the remaining loop. Complete the wraps.

3 Cut a 10-in. (25 cm) piece of wire. String a 16–22 mm bead and make a set of wraps (Basics) above it, leaving an 8-in. (20 cm) wire tail. Make the first half of a wrapped loop above the wraps. Make four large-bead units.

4 Cut 3 in. (7.6 cm) of wire. String a 6–15 mm bead and make a set of wraps. Make the first half of a wrapped loop above the wraps. Repeat with the remaining 6–15 mm beads.

5 Attach a large-bead unit to the end of the chain. Complete the wraps (see Wrapping, p. 67).

6 Attach the remaining bead units as desired, completing the wraps as you go.

Supplies

bracelet
- ◆ **4** 16–22 mm gemstones or glass beads, top drilled
- ◆ **6–10** 6–15 mm gemstones or glass beads, top drilled
- ◆ 8 mm oval bead
- ◆ 73–85 in. (1.9–2.2 m) 26-gauge half-hard wire
- ◆ 7–8 in. (18–20 cm) cable chain, 3–5 mm links
- ◆ lobster claw clasp
- ◆ chainnose and roundnose pliers
- ◆ diagonal wire cutters

earrings
- ◆ **2** 16–22 mm gemstones or glass beads, top drilled
- ◆ **4** 6–15 mm gemstones or glass beads, top drilled
- ◆ 32 in. (81 cm) 26-gauge half-hard wire
- ◆ 2 in. (5 cm) cable chain, 3–4 mm links
- ◆ pair of earring wires
- ◆ chainnose and roundnose pliers
- ◆ diagonal wire cutters

1 earrings • Cut a 1-in. (2.5 cm) piece of chain. Make a large-bead unit as in step 3 of the bracelet. Make two bead units as in step 4 of the bracelet.

2 Attach the large-bead unit to one end of the chain (Wrapping, p. 67). Attach the remaining bead units as desired, completing the wraps as you go (Basics, p. 12).

3 Open the loop of an earring wire (Basics). Attach the dangle and close the loop. Make a second earring to match the first.

Wrapping

1. Grasping the wrapped loop with chainnose pliers, use your fingers to wrap the wire around the top of the bead. Leave 1–2 in. (2.5–5 cm) for coiling.

2. Use roundnose pliers to make a small loop at the end of the wire.

3. Reposition the roundnose pliers across the loop and continue to coil the wire. Press it flat against the bead.

Design alternative

Strategic uniformity can be striking, too. Using black CZs, make the occasional silver dangles really pop.

Tip

• Arrange the dangles along the chain before attaching them to make sure you have a balanced arrangement of shapes and colors.

> "I love semiprecious stones, especially if they're roughly faceted. I love that rough elegance."

BLOCKS
of COLOR

Square and diamond-shaped beads form a geometric necklace and earrings

by Gia Amschel

To make blocks of color look dynamic, this necklace incorporates both organic and sparkling elements. Depending on the pendant you use, the result can be bold and modern or delicate and classic. To create your desired effect, use bicone crystals that mimic the shape of the pendant, in colors that complement the markings in the square beads.

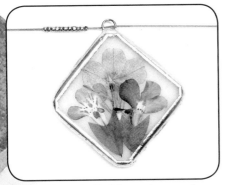

1 necklace • Cut two pieces of beading wire (Basics, p. 12). Over both wires, center a pendant. String ten to 15 11º seed beads until there are enough to make a bail.

2 On each side, over both ends, string a color A bicone crystal. Separate the pairs of wires and string two 11ºs over each pair.

3 On each side, over both ends, string: color B bicone crystal, square bead, color B bicone, square, color C bicone, square, color C bicone, square, color C bicone.

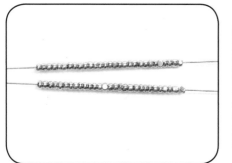

4 On each end, string 11ºs until the necklace is within 1 in. (2.5 cm) of the finished length.

5 On each side, over both ends, string a spacer, a crimp bead, a spacer, and half of a clasp. Check the fit, and add or remove beads from each end if necessary. Go back through the beads just strung and tighten the wires. Crimp the crimp beads (Basics) and trim the excess wire.

1 earrings · On a head pin, string a bicone crystal, a square bead, and a bicone in a second color. Make a wrapped loop (Basics, p. 12).

2 Open the loop of an earring wire (Basics). Attach the dangle and close the loop. Make a second earring to match the first.

Supplies

Pendant and square beads for the brown necklace and earrings available from Powder Horn Trading Co., (406) 752-6669.

necklace (brown 16½ in./ 41.9 cm; green 17 in./43 cm)
- 35–50 mm diamond-shaped pendant (floral pendant from Theresa Dart, lilystudios.net)
- **8** 10–14 mm square beads (serpentine beads from Chelsea's Beads, chelseasbeads.com)
- **11** 6 mm bicone crystals, **1** color A, **4** color B, **6** color C
- 2 g 11º seed beads
- **4** 3 mm round spacers
- flexible beading wire, .010 or .012
- **2** crimp beads
- toggle clasp
- chainnose or crimping pliers
- diagonal wire cutters

earrings
- **2** 10–14 mm square beads (serpentine beads from Chelsea's Beads, chelseasbeads.com)
- **4** 6 mm bicone crystals, **2** each in two colors
- **2** 2-in. (5 cm) head pins
- pair of earring wires
- chainnose and roundnose pliers
- diagonal wire cutters

Tip

For an array of colors, try a strand of square jasper beads.

Make a necklace
overlapping
with style

Tortoise-colored beads give a fresh edge to a quick necklace

by Rupa Balachandar

When you string corner-drilled beads with a couple of silver tubes in between, the slabs overlap beautifully. Use chocolate-hued chalcedony to complement fashion's trendy neutrals.

Supplies

All supplies from Rupa B. Designs, rupab.com.

necklace 20 in. (51 cm)
- 14½-in. (36.8 cm) strand 15–27 mm graduated rectangular beads, corner drilled
- **80–100** 4–5 mm Thai-silver tube beads
- flexible beading wire, .018 or .019
- **2** crimp beads
- toggle clasp
- chainnose or crimping pliers
- diagonal wire cutters

1 Cut a piece of beading wire (Basics, p. 12). Center the largest rectangular bead on the wire.

2 On each end, string two silver beads and the next-largest rectangle. Repeat until the strand is within 5 in. (13 cm) of the finished length.

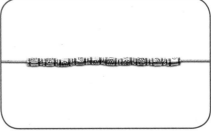

3 On each end, string silver beads until the strand is within 1 in. (2.5 cm) of the finished length.

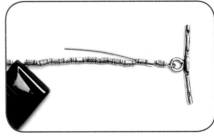

4 On each end, string a crimp bead, a silver bead, and half of a clasp. Check the fit, and add or remove beads from each end if necessary. Go back through the last few beads strung and tighten the wire. Crimp the crimp bead (Basics) and trim the excess wire.

This
look
is worth
the extra
effort

Filigree accents add charming details **by Roxanne Fraga**

Some occasions — and the jewelry that go with them — call for a special effort. This necklace shows you're prepared to go the extra mile to look gorgeous. So settle in with a good long movie and start wrapping those loops. Complete the look with matching earrings that you can make in a flash.

1 necklace • On a 2-in. (5 cm) head pin, string: faceted spacer, leaf bead cap, focal bead, leaf bead cap, crystal rondelle. Make the first half of a wrapped loop (Basics, p. 12).

2a Decide how long you want your necklace to be. Cut 14 to 18 ½-in. (1.3 cm) pieces of chain. To alter the length of the necklace, add or subtract pairs of chain.

b Cut a 3-in. (7.6 cm) piece of wire. Make the first half of a wrapped loop on one end. String a barrel bead and make the first half a wrapped loop. Make a bead unit for each chain.

3 Attach two pieces of chain to the loop of the pendant unit. Complete the wraps.

4 On each end, attach a barrel-bead unit and a chain. Complete the wraps. Continue attaching the remaining bead units and chains. Complete the wraps as you go, leaving the last loop unwrapped.

5 Check the fit, and add or remove bead units if necessary. On each end, attach half of a clasp to the unwrapped loop. Complete the wraps.

6 On a 1½-in. (3.8 cm) head pin, string a 6 mm round crystal, a 6 mm bead cap, and a 3 mm round spacer. Make the first half of a wrapped loop.

On a 1½-in. (3.8 cm) head pin, string a faceted spacer and a 6 mm rondelle. Make the first half of a wrapped loop.

On a 1½-in. (3.8 cm) head pin, string a 2 mm spacer and a 4 mm crystal. Make the first half of a wrapped loop. Repeat for each 4 mm crystal color.

Make one of each type of bead unit for every chain in the necklace.

7 Attach one of each bead unit to the links of each chain. Complete the wraps.

> **"**I've met many beginning beaders who lack confidence in their abilities. With a little encouragement they create beautiful jewelry.**"**

Supplies

necklace 17 in. (43 cm)
- 20–30 mm focal bead
- **14–18** 10 mm barrel beads
- **14–18** 6 mm rondelles
- **14–18** 6 mm round crystals
- 6 mm crystal rondelle
- **56–72** 4 mm round or bicone crystals, in four colors
- **15–19** 3 mm faceted spacers
- **14–18** 3 mm round spacers
- **56–72** 2 mm round spacers
- **14–18** 6 mm bead caps
- **2** filigree leaf bead caps (Shipwreck Beads, 800.950.4232, shipwreckbeads.com)
- 4 ft. (1.2 m) 22-gauge half-hard wire

- 8–10 in. (20–25 cm) cable chain, 3 mm links
- 2-in. (5 cm) head pin
- **84–108** 1½-in. (3.8 cm) head pins
- toggle clasp
- chainnose and roundnose pliers
- diagonal wire cutters

earrings
- **2** 10 mm barrel beads
- **2** 6 mm round crystals
- **2** 4 mm round or bicone crystals
- **2** 3 mm round spacers
- **2** 2 mm round spacers
- **2** 6 mm bead caps
- 3 in. (7.6 cm) 22-gauge half-hard wire
- **4** 1½-in. (3.8 cm) head pins
- pair of earring wires
- chainnose and roundnose pliers
- diagonal wire cutters

1 earrings • On a 1½-in. (3.8 cm) head pin, string a 6 mm round crystal, a bead cap, and a 3 mm round spacer. Make the first half of a wrapped loop (Basics, p. 12).

On a 1½-in. (3.8 cm) head pin, string a 2 mm spacer and a 4 mm crystal. Make the first half of a wrapped loop.

Cut a 1½-in. (3.8 cm) piece of wire. Make a plain loop (Basics) on one end. String a barrel bead and make a plain loop.

2 Attach each crystal unit to a plain loop of the barrel-bead unit. Complete the wraps.

Open the loop of an earring wire (Basics). Attach the dangle and close the loop. Make a second earring to match the first.

Tip

You can buy strands that include both barrel beads and rondelles. Try Fire Mountain Gems and Beads, firemountaingems.com, or Chic Beads, 562.431.6332.

Design alternative

For a little less effort (and expense!), use longer chains between the tube beads and limit the crystal clusters to the front of the necklace.

Supersize a
necklace with
turquoise and
howlite nuggets

by Carol McKinney

Texas-sized

Turquoise, my favorite gemstone, makes a great starting point for a huge-bead necklace inspired by my home state. Just mix in gaspeite and howlite for a bright assortment of colors. For a beautiful finish, you can use decorative earring components. Just make sure they're strong enough to support the heavy strands.

1 **necklace** • Cut three pieces of beading wire (Basics, p. 12). On one wire, center beads as desired.

2 String nuggets on each end, interspersing round beads, until the strand is within 3 in. (7.6 cm) of the finished length.

3 String beads as desired on the remaining two wires until each strand is within 3 in. (7.6 cm) of the finished length.

4 On each end of each wire, string a spacer, a crimp bead, a spacer, and the corresponding loop of a three-to-one connector. Check the fit, allowing 1 in. (2.5 cm) for the clasp. Add or remove beads if necessary. Go back through the beads just strung and tighten the wires. Crimp the crimp beads (Basics) and trim the excess wire.

three strand

5 On each end, attach a split ring (Basics). On one end, attach a lobster claw clasp to the split ring.

6 On a head pin, string a bead. Make the first half of a wrapped loop (Basics). Attach the dangle to one of the split rings and complete the wraps.

1 earrings • On a head pin, string a nugget and a bead cap. Make a plain loop (Basics, p. 12).

2 Open the loop of an earring wire (Basics) and attach the dangle. Close the loop. Make a second earring to match the first.

Design alternative

For an earthier take on turquoise, mix in bronze pearls and jasper in light- and dark-brown shades.

Supplies

necklace 20½ in. (52.1 cm)
- 16-in. (41 cm) strand 20–30 mm nuggets
- 16-in. (41 cm) strand 15–20 mm nuggets
- 16-in. (41 cm) strand 14–16 mm round beads
- 16-in. (41 cm) strand 8 mm round beads
- **12** 3–4 mm round spacers
- flexible beading wire, .018 or .019
- **2** three-to-one connectors
- 2-in. (5 cm) head pin
- **2** 5–6 mm split rings
- **6** crimp beads
- lobster claw clasp
- chainnose and roundnose pliers
- diagonal wire cutters
- crimping pliers (optional)
- split-ring pliers (optional)

earrings
- **2** 15–20 mm nuggets
- **2** 8–12 mm bead caps
- **2** 1½-in. (3.8 cm) head pins
- pair of lever-back earring wires
- chainnose and roundnose pliers
- diagonal wire cutters

Tip

String or substitute additional 8 mm round beads if you need to alter a strand's length only slightly.

Quick silver

Complex shapes add drama to a simple design

by Carol McKinney

The design is timeless and the stringing takes no time at all. What could be better? Just let these irregularly shaped silver nuggets take center stage, add gemstones (turquoise is silver's best friend) or ceramic ovals, and you're done. The matching earring options are a snap, too.

1 necklace • Cut a piece of beading wire (Basics, p. 12). Center a 4-in. (10 cm) section of silver beads, alternating between 13–17 mm nuggets and 9 mm nuggets. End with a 13–17 mm nugget.

2 On each end, string oval beads until the necklace is within 1 in. (2.5 cm) of the finished length. String two or three 9 mm nuggets, a crimp bead, and half of a clasp. Check the fit, and add or remove beads if necessary. Go back through a few beads and tighten the wire. Crimp the crimp beads (Basics) and trim the excess wire.

"At first, I was making things too complicated. I finally just strung some turquoise with the silver and it turned out great — as simple as it is."

Design alternative

Create strong visual impact with a few silver beads placed off-center and dramatic black beads.

1 long earrings • On a head pin, string an oval bead, a 13 mm nugget, and an oval bead. Make a plain loop (Basics, p. 12).

2 Open the loop of an earring wire (Basics). Attach the dangle and close the loop. Make a second earring to match the first.

1 short earrings • On a head pin, string a 9 mm nugget, an oval bead, and a nugget. Make a wrapped loop (Basics, p. 12).

2 Open the loop of an earring wire (Basics). Attach the dangle and close the loop. Make a second earring to match the first.

Supplies

Silver beads from Rings & Things, rings-things.com. Ceramic beads from Clay River Designs, clayriverdesigns.com (click on "etcetera" and then on "melon ovals").

necklace 17 in. (43 cm)
- **9–13** 13–17 mm hollow Karen Hill Tribe silver nuggets in assorted shapes
- **16-in. (41 cm) strand** 13–15 mm oval beads
- **12–16** 9 mm silver nuggets
- flexible beading wire, .014 or .015
- **2** crimp beads
- toggle clasp
- chainnose or crimping pliers
- diagonal wire cutters

long earrings
- **4** 13–15 mm oval beads
- **2** 13 mm hollow rectangular Karen Hill Tribe silver nuggets
- **2** 2½-in. (6.4 cm) head pins
- pair of earring wires
- chainnose and roundnose pliers
- diagonal wire cutters

short earrings
- **2** 13–15 mm oval beads
- **4** 9 mm silver nuggets
- **2** 2½-in. (6.4 cm) head pins
- pair of earring wires
- chainnose and roundnose pliers
- diagonal wire cutters

Tips

• Arrange the different shapes of the larger silver nuggets in the desired order before you string them.
• If you like, attach a decorative oval bead to the loop half of the clasp.

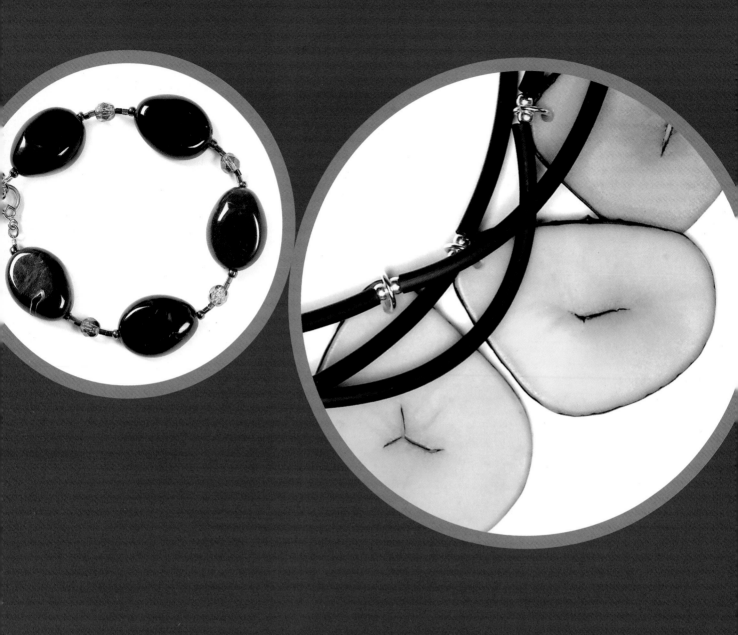

Mixed

media

KEYS

to the past

Jewelry can unlock
a personal memory

by Jane Konkel

Mrs. Knitter, a fourth-grade teacher at my elementary school, was a tough old bird. A heavy set of keys hung from her substantial hips, so we could hear her approach from three classrooms away. My key bracelet conjures up a vivid recollection, but even if you didn't know Mrs. Knitter, keys are a primary fashion motif, opening doors all over trinket town. While you're designing your jewelry, ponder your key memories.

1 necklace • Cut a 2½-in. (6.4 cm) piece of wire. Make the first half of a wrapped loop (Basics, p. 12). String a rondelle. Make the first half of a wrapped loop. Make four rondelle units.

Make two round-bead units, stringing a flat spacer, a round bead, and a flat spacer.

2 Cut four 3-in. (7.6 cm) pieces of chain. String a key on one piece. Attach both ends and one loop of a rondelle unit. Complete the wraps.

3 Attach both ends of another piece of chain and the rondelle unit's remaining loop. Attach the center link of chain to a loop of a round-bead unit. Complete the wraps as you go.

4 String a saucer on a piece of chain. Attach both ends and the round-bead unit's remaining loop. Complete the wraps.

5 **a** String another piece of chain through the saucer. Attach both ends and one loop of a rondelle unit. Complete the wraps. Leave the remaining loop unwrapped.

b Repeat steps 2–5a on the other side.

6 Cut a 6–8-in. (15–20 cm) piece of large-link chain. Attach each end to an unwrapped loop. Check the fit, making sure the necklace fits over your head. Trim chain if necessary. Complete the wraps.

1 bracelet • Cut a piece of beading wire (Basics, p. 12). String beads until the bracelet is within 3 in. (7.6 cm) of the finished length.

2 Attach one split ring to a key and one to a clasp (Basics).

3 On each end of the beading wire, string a crimp bead and a split ring. Check the fit, and add or remove beads if necessary. Go back through a few beads and tighten the wire. Crimp the crimp bead (Basics) and trim the excess wire. If desired, close a crimp cover over each crimp bead (Basics).

Supplies

necklace 20 in. (51 cm)
- 60 mm Lucite key (Ornamentea, ornamentea.com)
- **2** 30 mm large-hole resin saucers (Chelsea's Beads chelseasbeads.com)
- **2** 10 mm round resin beads (Rings & Things, rings-things.com)
- **4** 6 mm fire-polished crystal rondelles
- **4** 5–6 mm flat spacers
- 15 in. (38 cm) 24-gauge half-hard wire
- 25 in. (64 cm) chain, 3–4 mm links
- 6–8 in. (15–20 cm) chain, 5–6 mm links
- chainnose and roundnose pliers
- diagonal wire cutters

bracelet
- 60 mm Lucite key (Ornamentea, ornamentea.com)
- **2–4** 14 mm square resin beads (Jo-Ann Stores, 888.739.4120, joann.com)
- **2–4** 14 mm diamond-shaped resin beads (Chelsea's Beads, chelseasbeads.com)

- **7–9** 6 mm fire-polished crystal rondelles
- **3–5** 10 mm flat spacers
- flexible beading wire, .018 or .019
- **2** 12 mm split rings
- **2** crimp beads
- **2** crimp covers (optional)
- 32 mm pager clip clasp (Rings & Things, rings-things.com)
- split-ring and crimping pliers
- diagonal wire cutters
- chainnose pliers (optional)

earrings
- **2** 22 mm keys (Jo-Ann Stores, joann.com)
- **2** 14 mm diamond-shaped resin beads (Chelsea's Beads, chelseasbeads.com)
- **2** 6 mm fire-polished crystal rondelles
- **2** 10 mm flat spacers
- 5 in. (13 cm) 24-gauge half-hard wire
- pair of earring wires
- chainnose and roundnose pliers
- diagonal wire cutters

1 earrings • Cut a 2½-in. (6.4 cm) piece of wire. Make the first half of a wrapped loop (Basics, p. 12). String a key and complete the wraps.

2 String a rondelle, a spacer, and a diamond-shaped bead. Make a wrapped loop.

3 Open the loop of an earring wire (Basics). Attach the dangle and close the loop. Make a second earring in the mirror image of the first.

Design alternatives

Try a necklace with a beaded strand and toggle clasp. The Lucite key, brass chain, and clasp are from Ornamentea.

Wear the bracelet on a belt loop at your hip, Mrs.-Knitter style. Clasp from Jewelry Supply Inc. (jewelrysupply.com).

"I like using timeworn skeleton keys in jewelry, but I couldn't resist the icy colors of these Lucite ones. They don't make Mrs. Knitter's warning sound, and that's reassuring.**"**

Transform

dressy

eftover beads into
jewelry

The right mix of beads gives a necklace-and-earring set cohesive style • **by Ali Otterbein**

I'm only 15, but I've been surrounded by beads my entire life, especially since my parents turned the first floor of our house into a bead store a few years ago. Living above a bead store gives me lots of gemstones, pearls, crystals, and glass to choose from, but you can be just as creative using your stash of leftover beads.

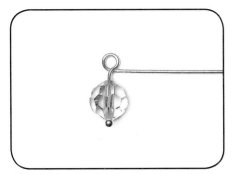

1 **necklace** • To make a bead unit: On a head pin, string a bead and make the first half of a wrapped loop (Basics, p. 12). Make a total of 35 to 50 3–10 mm bead units. Set aside eight 3–4 mm bead units and 12 5–6 mm bead units for step 7.

2 To make a top-drilled–bead unit: Cut a 3-in. (7.6 cm) piece of wire. String a top-drilled bead and make a set of wraps above it (Basics). Make the first half of a wrapped loop. Make as many top-drilled–bead units as desired.

3 To make a focal-bead unit: On a head pin, string a focal bead and a bead cap. Make the first half of a wrapped loop.

4 To make a pendant: Cut a 1-in. (2.5 cm) piece of chain. Attach the focal-bead unit to one end and complete the wraps. Attach two to four bead units to each chain link, completing the wraps as you go. Attach the largest bead units near the bottom of the chain.

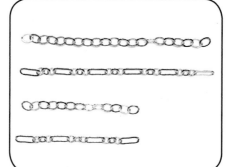

5 Cut six 2-in. (5 cm) pieces of chain, three each in two styles. Cut two 1½-in. (3.8 cm) pieces of chain, one each in two styles.

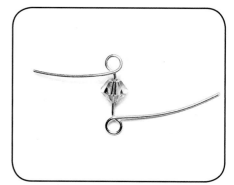

6 Cut a 3-in. (7.6 cm) piece of wire. Make the first half of a wrapped loop on one end. String a 3–5 mm bead and make the first half of a wrapped loop. Make a total of nine to 11 units.

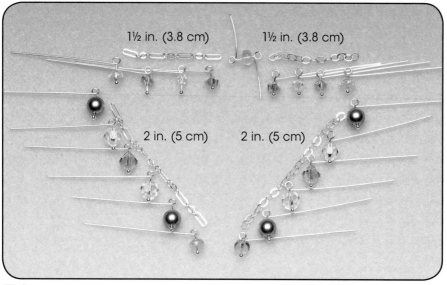

1½ in. (3.8 cm) 1½ in. (3.8 cm)

2 in. (5 cm) 2 in. (5 cm)

7 On your work space, arrange six 5–6 mm bead units along each 2-in. (5 cm) chain and four 3–4 mm bead units along each 1½-in. (3.8 cm) chain. A bead unit from step 6 will connect the two short chains.

8 Attach the bead units to the chains, completing the wraps as you go.

Use bead units from step 6 to attach one end of each 2-in. (5 cm) chain and one 8–9 mm jump ring. Use a bead unit to attach the pendant and the 8–9 mm jump ring. Use a bead unit to connect the two 1½-in. (3.8 cm) chains.

9 Open a 4 mm jump ring (Basics) and attach a 2-in. (5 cm) chain. Close the jump ring. Repeat on the other 2-in. (5 cm) chain.

Use a 4 mm jump ring to attach each 1½-in. (3.8 cm) chain to a closed jump ring.

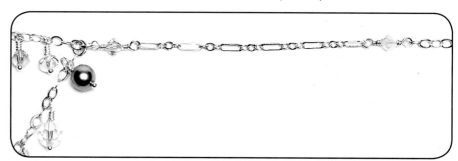

10 On each end, use a bead unit to attach a 2-in. (5 cm) chain to the second 4 mm jump ring. Complete the wraps. Use a bead unit to attach another 2-in. (5 cm) chain to each end. Complete the wraps.

Supplies

necklace (orange 19½ in./49.5 cm; purple 21 in./53 cm

- 15–20 mm focal bead
- **2-4** 10–14 mm beads, top drilled
- **5-6** 7–10 mm beads
- **18-27** 5–6 mm beads
- **23-28** 3–4 mm beads
- 8–10 mm bead cap
- 39–51 in. (.9–1.3 m) 24-gauge half-hard wire
- 16–20 in. (41–51 cm) chain, 3–5 mm links, in two styles
- **36-51** 1½-in. (3.8 cm) decorative head pins
- **4** 4 mm jump rings
- 8–9 mm soldered jump ring
- S-hook clasp and **2** 5–7 mm soldered jump rings
- chainnose and roundnose pliers
- diagonal wire cutters

earrings

- **2-4** 10–14 mm beads, top drilled
- **10-12** 7–10 mm beads
- **10-14** 5–6 mm beads
- **10-12** 3–4 mm beads
- 12–18 in. (30–46 cm) 24-gauge half-hard wire
- 1½ in. (3.8 cm) chain, 3–5 mm links
- **30-38** 1½-in. (3.8cm) decorative head pins
- pair of earring wires
- chainnose and roundnose pliers
- diagonal wire cutters

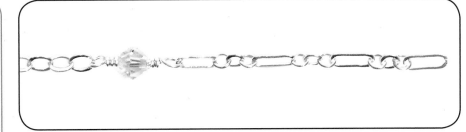

11 Check the fit. To shorten the necklace, trim chain from each end. To lengthen it, cut a piece of chain for each end, one in each style, and then use a bead unit to attach a chain to each end.

12 On each end, use a bead unit to attach a 5–7 mm soldered jump ring. On one end, attach an S-hook clasp. Close one side of the clasp with chainnose pliers.

Tips

- As you attach the chains to the necklace, alternate the two chain styles.
- After step 10, your necklace will be about 16 in. (41 cm). If you want a shorter necklace, make only nine bead units in step 6. If you want a longer necklace, make 11 bead units.

1 earrings · Follow steps 1 and 2 of the necklace to make 15 to 20 bead units.

Cut a ¾-in. (1.9 cm) piece of chain. Attach the largest bead unit to one end. Complete the wraps.

2 Attach two to four bead units to each chain link, completing the wraps as you go. Attach the largest bead units near the bottom of the chain.

3 Follow step 6 of the necklace to make a bead unit. Attach a loop of the bead unit to the dangle. Attach the remaining loop to the loop of an earring wire. Complete the wraps. Make a second earring to match the first.

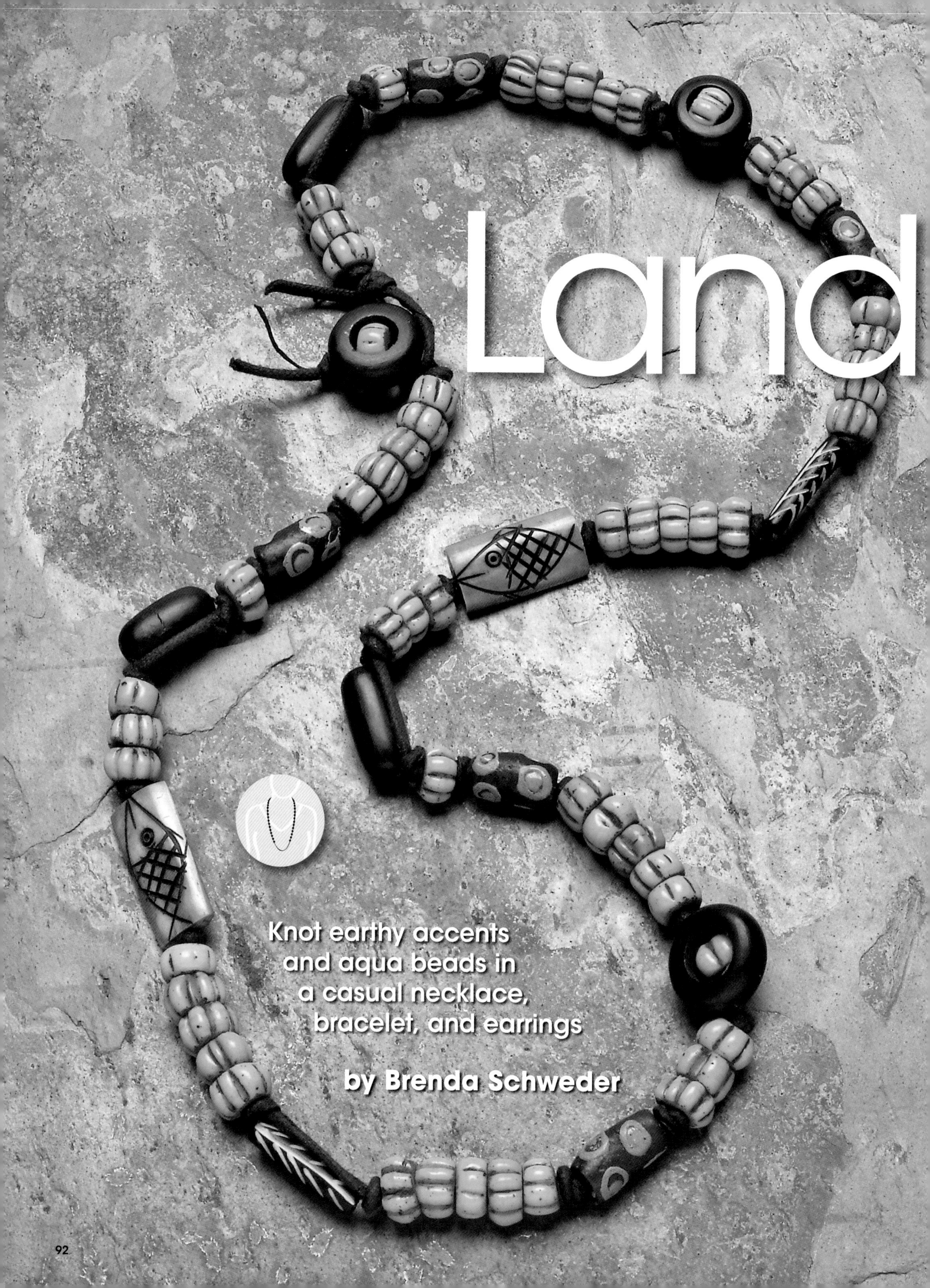

Land

Knot earthy accents
and aqua beads in
a casual necklace,
bracelet, and earrings

by Brenda Schweder

Blue melon-shaped beads bring a touch of ocean to natural materials like bone, clay, and wood. If you're not in a seafaring mood, try a strand of African trade beads in assorted colors.

& sea

1 necklace • Cut 6 ft. (1.8 m) each of cord and thread. Leaving a 1-in. (2.5 cm) tail, tie an overhand knot (Basics, p. 12) with both pieces.

2 On the thread, string the first hole of a donut bead, a melon-shaped bead, and the second hole of the donut. Tie a knot with both pieces.

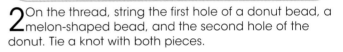

3 Over both pieces, string five melons and tie a knot. String a rectangular or tube-shaped accent bead and tie a knot. String a melon and tie a knot.

On the thread, string an accent bead. Tie a knot with both pieces. Over both pieces, string three melons and tie a knot. String an accent bead and tie a knot.

4 Over both pieces, string five melons and tie a knot. On the thread, string an accent bead. Tie a knot with both pieces. Over both pieces, string five melons and tie a knot. String an accent bead and tie a knot. String three melons and tie a knot.

Repeat steps 2–4 until the necklace is within 1 in. (2.5 cm) of the finished length, ending with a knot.

5 Wrap the thread around the cord twice. Make a 1-in. (2.5 cm) loop and loosely tie a knot with both pieces. Make sure the loop fits around the donut at the other end of the necklace. Tighten the knot and trim the excess cord and thread.

bracelet • Cut 2 ft. (61 cm) each of cord and thread. Leaving a 1-in. (2.5 cm) tail, tie an overhand knot (Basics, p. 12) with both pieces. Follow steps 2 and 3 of the necklace. Over both pieces, string melons until the bracelet is within 1 in. (2.5 cm) of the finished length, and tie a knot. Follow step 5 to finish.

Supply Notes

I used a variety of sources for these projects:
• Beads and Pieces, beadsandpieces. com for accent beads
• Kamol, info@kamol.com for blue melon-shaped beads
• Rings & Things, rings-things.com for waxed cotton cord
• Royalwood Ltd., royalwoodltd.com for waxed linen thread

1 earrings • About ⅛ in. (3 mm) from the decorative end of a head pin, make a right-angle bend. Wrap the wire around a jaw of your roundnose pliers .

Supplies

necklace 31½ in. (80 cm)
◆ **12–15** 20–30 mm rectangular and tube-shaped accent beads
◆ **3** 20 mm wood donut beads, side drilled
◆ **55–68** 10 mm melon-shaped beads
◆ 6 ft. (1.8 m) waxed cotton cord, 2 mm diameter
◆ 6 ft. (1.8 m) waxed linen thread, 0.5 mm diameter

bracelet
◆ **3** 20–30 mm rectangular and tube-shaped accent beads
◆ 20 mm wood donut bead, side drilled
◆ **12–15** 10 mm melon-shaped beads
◆ 2 ft. (61 cm) waxed cotton cord, 2 mm diameter
◆ 2 ft. (61 cm) waxed linen thread, 0.5 mm diameter

earrings
◆ **2** 20 mm wood donut beads, side drilled
◆ **2** 10 mm melon-shaped beads
◆ 6 in. (15 cm) waxed cotton cord, 2 mm diameter
◆ 6 in. (15 cm) waxed linen thread, 0.5 mm diameter
◆ **2** 2½-in. (6.4 cm) decorative head pins
◆ chainnose and roundnose pliers
◆ diagonal wire cutters
◆ bench block or anvil
◆ hammer
◆ metal file or emery board

2 Bend the wire around a pen barrel. Use chainnose pliers to make a slight upward bend in the wire end. Trim the excess wire and file the end.

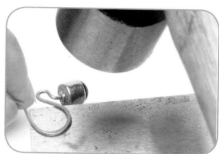

3 On a bench block or anvil, hammer the earring wire. Flip the earring wire over and hammer the other side.

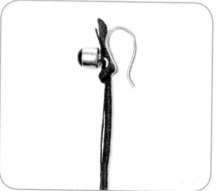

4 Cut 6 in. (15 cm) each of cord and thread. Leaving a ½-in. (1.3 cm) tail, tie a loose overhand knot (Basics, p. 12) with both pieces. String the knot on the earring wire, and tighten the knot.

5 On the thread, string the first hole of a donut bead, a melon-shaped bead, and the second hole of the donut. Tie a knot with both pieces. Trim the pieces to different lengths. Make a second earring to match the first.

Tip

If you have trouble stringing the cord and thread through a bead's hole, twist the ends together and trim them diagonally.

Flower field
bracelet

These double-drilled beads are perfect for a cuff

by Jean Yates

When I received these double-drilled beads from ceramic-bead artist Melanie Brooks Lukacs, I knew they were destined to become a cuff-style bracelet. Melanie aptly calls the design "flower field" because upon closer inspection, tiny jonquils reveal themselves.

1 bracelet • Cut two pieces of beading wire (Basics, p. 12). On each wire, string a bicone crystal, a spacer, the corresponding hole of a rectangular bead, a spacer, and a bicone. Repeat four times.

2 On each end of each wire, string a bicone, a spacer, a crimp bead, and the corresponding loop of half of a clasp. Check the fit, and add or remove beads from each end if necessary. Go back through the last few beads strung and tighten the wires. Crimp the crimp beads (Basics) and trim the excess wire.

Supplies

bracelet
- **5** 25 mm rectangular tile beads, double drilled (Earthenwood Studio, earthenwoodstudio.com)
- **24–32** 4 mm bicone crystals
- **24** 4 mm round spacers
- flexible beading wire, .014 or .015
- **4** crimp beads
- two-strand toggle clasp
- chainnose or crimping pliers
- diagonal wire cutters

earrings
- **2** 22 mm square tile beads with two loops (Earthenwood Studio)
- **22** 4 mm bicone crystals
- **22** 1½-in. (3.8 cm) decorative head pins
- pair of earring wires
- chainnose and roundnose pliers
- diagonal wire cutters

Tip

To make your bracelet longer, string additional bicone crystals on the end of each wire until the bracelet is within 1 in. (2.5 cm) of the finished length.

Design alternative

With **35 colors** of tile beads to choose from, picking just one may be difficult. Try a variety. In this bracelet, I chose a range to resemble Fiesta dinnerware. A pair of fairy-bead earrings complement the color array.

1 earrings • On a decorative head pin, string a bicone crystal. Make the first half of a wrapped loop (Basics, p. 12). Make 11 bicone units.

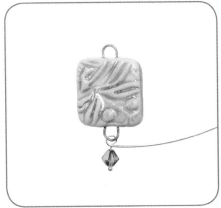

2 Attach the bicone unit to the loop of a square bead and complete the wraps.

3 Attach the remaining bead units, completing the wraps as you go.

4 Open the loop of an earring wire (Basics). Attach the dangle and close the loop. Make a second earring to match the first.

❝I have two children with autism. They add a sense of wonder to my life and inspire me to grow in every aspect of my creative process.❞

Botanical bracelet

Whip up a seasonal bracelet and earrings

by Nina Cooper

Intricate leaves flutter on a lightweight charm bracelet and subtle earrings. In your version, dangle fragments of color with beads in summer aquas or autumn browns. Either color combination will harmonize with your nature-inspired design.

1 bracelet • On a decorative head pin, string a bead. Make the first half of a wrapped loop (Basics, p. 12). Make ten to 12 bead units.

2 Decide how long you want your bracelet to be and cut a piece of chain to that length. Attach a bead unit to the center link and complete the wraps.

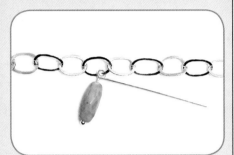

3 Open a 4 mm jump ring (Basics) and attach a charm to a link. Close the jump ring. Attach the remaining bead units and charms to different links.

4 Check the fit, allowing 1 in. (2.5 cm) for finishing. Trim links if necessary. On each end, use a 5 mm jump ring to attach half of a toggle clasp.

1 earrings • Cut a 2-in. (5 cm) piece of wire. Make the first half of a wrapped loop (Basics, p. 12) on one end. Attach a charm and complete the wraps.

2 String a bead. Make a wrapped loop perpendicular to the first loop.

3 Open the loop of an earring wire (Basics) and attach the dangle. Close the loop. Make a second earring to match the first.

Supplies

Silver and gold charms, chain, clasps, and findings from Nina Designs, ninadesigns.com.

bracelet
- **8** 10–16 mm leaf charms
- **10–12** 10–12 mm tube or oval beads, in three or four colors
- 6½–8 in. (16.5–20 cm) flat cable chain, 6–8 mm links
- **10–12** 2-in. (5 cm) decorative head pins
- **2** 5 mm jump rings
- **8** 4 mm jump rings
- toggle clasp
- chainnose and roundnose pliers
- diagonal wire cutters

earrings
- **2** 10–16 mm leaf charms
- **2** 10–12 mm tube or oval beads
- 4 in. (10 cm) 24-gauge half-hard wire
- pair of earring wires
- chainnose and roundnose pliers
- diagonal wire cutters

Chic
nuggets

Chunky Lucite nuggets look surprisingly refined with crystals and fancy chain

by Maria Camera

Despite their rugged shape, these lightweight Lucite beads have a distinctly delicate air. A 12-nugget strand is enough for a necklace, bracelet, and earrings, so the cost won't weigh you down either.

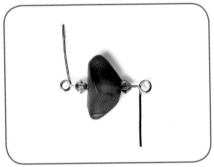

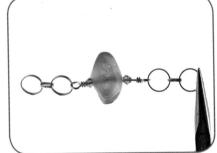

1 necklace • Cut a 3-in. (7.6 cm) piece of wire. Make the first half of a wrapped loop (Basics, p. 12). String a bicone crystal, a nugget, and a bicone. Make the first half of a wrapped loop. Make nine nugget units.

2 Cut ten ½-in. (1.3 cm) pieces of chain. Attach a chain to each loop of the largest nugget unit and complete the wraps.

3 On each end, continue attaching the remaining nugget units and chains, completing the wraps as you go. Check the fit and trim chain if necessary.

On each end, open a jump ring (Basics) and attach half of a clasp. Close the jump ring.

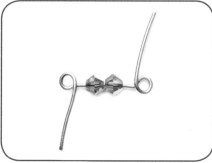

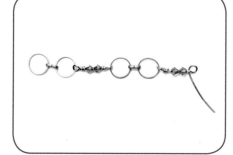

1 bracelet • Cut a 2-in. (5 cm) piece of wire. Make the first half of a wrapped loop (Basics, p. 12). String two bicone crystals. Make the first half of a wrapped loop. Make four bicone units.

Make a nugget unit following necklace step 1.

2 Cut two ½-in. (1.3 cm) pieces of chain. Attach a chain, a bicone unit, a chain, and a bicone unit. Complete the wraps, leaving the end loop unwrapped. Repeat to make a second strand.

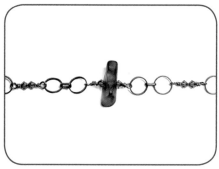

3 Attach each strand to a loop of the nugget unit. Complete the wraps.

4 On each end, attach half of a clasp and complete the wraps.

Supplies

Sterling silver chain available from Amidhara Gems & Minerals, amidhara.com. Copper chain available from Ornamentea, ornamentea.com.

necklace (silver necklaces 19 in./ 48 cm; copper 17 in./43 cm)
- 5-in. (13 cm) strand 10–21 mm Lucite nuggets (Art & Soul Beads, artandsoulbeads.com)
- **18** 4 mm bicone crystals
- 27 in. (69 cm) 24-gauge half-hard wire
- 8–10 in. (20–25 cm) fancy chain, 5–8 mm links
- **2** 5 mm jump rings
- clasp
- chainnose and roundnose pliers
- diagonal wire cutters

bracelet 7 in. (18 cm)
- 10–21 mm Lucite nugget (Art & Soul Beads, artandsoulbeads.com)
- **10** 4 mm bicone crystals
- 11 in. (28 cm) 24-gauge half-hard wire
- 3–4 in. (7.6–10 cm) fancy chain, 5–8 mm links
- clasp
- chainnose and roundnose pliers
- diagonal wire cutters

earrings
- **2** 10–21 mm Lucite nuggets (Art & Soul Beads, artandsoulbeads.com)
- **4** 4 mm bicone crystals
- **2** 2-in. (5 cm) head pins
- pair of earring wires
- chainnose and roundnose pliers
- diagonal wire cutters

❝I won't make jewelry I wouldn't wear. I want our jewelry to be pretty, classic, and reasonably priced.❞

1 earrings • On a head pin, string a bicone crystal, a nugget, and a bicone. Make a wrapped loop (Basics, p. 12).

2 Open the loop of an earring wire (Basics). Attach the nugget unit and close the loop. Make a second earring to match the first.

Tips

• Before you begin stringing, choose the largest nugget for the center of the necklace. Pick out the two most similar nuggets for earrings, and then pair the rest of the nuggets by size and shape for a symmetrical strand. An "odd" nugget shape is perfect for the bracelet.

• Adjust the length of the necklace or bracelet by cutting the chain pieces shorter or longer.

• If the holes in the Lucite nuggets are too large for the 4 mm bicone crystals, string a seed bead or two into the holes so the bicones remain visible.

Design alternative

Despite their conventional shape, round Lucite beads look edgy when you combine two moody colors with gunmetal findings.

The wonders of plastic

Bodacious baubles float in a lightweight set

by Jennifer Ortiz

It's hard to believe these gorgeous beads are plastic. Their beauty lies in both their opaque colors and translucent finishes. What's more, you can get a heavy-duty look by stringing just a few beads. They're relatively inexpensive and widely available. Search for acrylic, Bakelite, Catalin, celluloid, Lucite, and resin vintage versions.

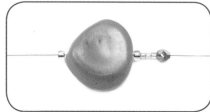

1 necklace • Cut a piece of beading wire (Basics, p. 12). String: large seed bead, color A nugget bead, large seed bead, three small seed beads, 6 mm crystal.

2a String three small seed beads, a large seed bead, and a color B nugget bead.

 b Repeat the patterns in steps 1 and 2a, alternating color C, A, and B nuggets, until the strand is within 2 in. (5 cm) of the finished length. End with a nugget.

3 On each end, string: large seed bead, three small seed beads, crimp bead, small seed bead, half of a clasp. Check the fit, and add or remove beads if necessary. Go back through the last few beads strung and tighten the wire. Crimp the crimp bead (Basics) and trim the excess wire.

1 bracelet • Cut a piece of beading wire (Basics, p. 12). String a seed bead, a color C nugget bead, a seed bead, and a 6 mm crystal. Repeat, alternating the nugget colors, until the strand is within 2 in. (5 cm) of the finished length. End with a nugget.

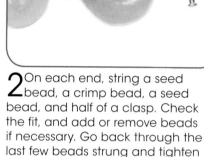

2 On each end, string a seed bead, a crimp bead, a seed bead, and half of a clasp. Check the fit, and add or remove beads if necessary. Go back through the last few beads strung and tighten the wire. Crimp the crimp bead (Basics) and trim the excess wire.

1 earrings • On a head pin, string a seed bead and a nugget bead. Make the first half of a wrapped loop (Basics, p. 12).

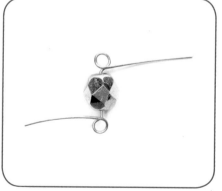

2 Cut a 2½-in. (6.4 cm) piece of wire. Make the first half of a wrapped loop. String a 6 mm crystal and make the first half of a wrapped loop.

3 Attach the nugget unit and a loop of the 6 mm unit to a soldered jump ring. Complete the wraps, leaving the top loop of the 6 mm unit unwrapped.

4 Attach the remaining loop to a jump ring and complete the wraps.

Open the loop of an earring wire (Basics) and attach the dangle. Close the loop. Make a second earring to match the first.

Design alternative

Dangle a solitary bead from an otherwise monochromatic bracelet.

> **"What inspires me most is seeing how people play with color in the clothing they wear. It gives me ideas about what colors work well together."**

Supplies

Small nuggets from Oriental Trading Co., orientaltrading.com. Large resin nuggets from Natural Touch Beads, naturaltouchbeads.com.

necklace (small-bead necklace 26 in./66 cm, large-bead necklace 31 in./79 cm)
- ◆ **12–18** 25–30 mm nuggets in three colors
- ◆ **11–17** 6 mm fire-polished crystals
- ◆ 1 g 6º (large) seed beads
- ◆ 2 g 11º (small) seed beads
- ◆ flexible beading wire, .014 or .015
- ◆ **2** crimp beads
- ◆ toggle clasp
- ◆ chainnose or crimping pliers
- ◆ diagonal wire cutters

bracelet
- ◆ **5** 25–30 mm nuggets in three colors
- ◆ **4** 6 mm fire-polished crystals
- ◆ **12–25** 6º or 11º seed beads
- ◆ flexible beading wire, .014 or .015
- ◆ **2** crimp beads
- ◆ toggle clasp
- ◆ chainnose or crimping pliers
- ◆ diagonal wire cutters

earrings
- ◆ **2** 25–30 mm nuggets
- ◆ **2** 6 mm fire-polished crystals
- ◆ **2** 6º or 11º seed beads
- ◆ 5 in. (13 cm) 24-gauge half-hard wire
- ◆ **2** 2½-in. (6.4 cm) head pins
- ◆ **4** 4 mm soldered jump rings
- ◆ pair of earring wires
- ◆ chainnose and roundnose pliers
- ◆ diagonal wire cutters

Tip

Make sure the seed beads are large enough that they don't slip through the holes of the nuggets.

Copper craze

Create custom links to accent a pendant

by Miachelle DePiano

Copper-accented jewelry is back in the fashion forefront. That's good news for jewelry artists, because copper wire is easy to work with and relatively inexpensive. Form copper wire links to connect an earthy pendant to soft leather lace. For simplicity, skip the clasp and just tie the ends.

Supplies

necklaces 32 in. (81 cm)

- 45–50 mm copper pendant
- 4 10–12 mm flat copper beads
- 34 in. (86 cm) 16-gauge half-hard copper wire
- 8 in. (20 cm) 22-gauge half-hard copper wire
- 20–30 in. (51–76 cm) suede lace
- 2 9–11 mm 16-gauge copper jump rings (Ornamentea, ornamentea.com)
- chainnose and roundnose pliers
- diagonal wire cutters

1 Cut a 2-in. (5 cm) piece of 16-gauge wire. On one end, make a plain loop (Basics, p. 12). String a pendant and make a plain loop.

2 To make bead units: Cut four 2-in. (5 cm) pieces of 16-gauge wire. On one end of each wire, use the largest part of your roundnose pliers to make a loop. String a flat bead and make a loop in the opposite direction.

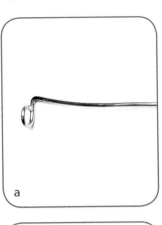

a

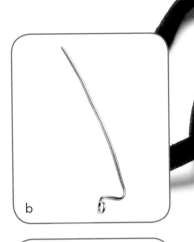

b

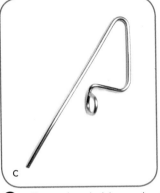

c

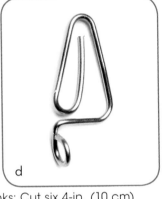

d

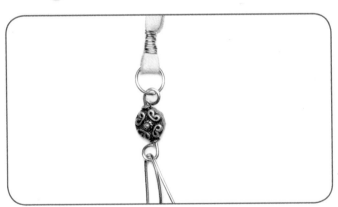

3 **a** To make six triangular links: Cut six 4-in. (10 cm) pieces of 16-gauge wire. On one end of each wire, use the largest part of your roundnose pliers to make a loop. Make a right-angle bend above each loop.

b On each wire, place the largest part of your roundnose pliers ½ in. (1.3 cm) from the bend and pull the wire up as shown.

c On each wire, place the pliers ¾ in. (1.9 cm) from the last bend and pull the wire down as shown.

d On each wire, place the pliers ¾ in. (1.9 cm) from the last bend, and pull the wire up as shown. Trim the excess wire.

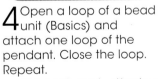

4 Open a loop of a bead unit (Basics) and attach one loop of the pendant. Close the loop. Repeat.

On each end, attach a link to the remaining loop.

5 On each side, open the loop of a link and attach the previous link. Repeat.

On each side, attach a bead unit. Open a jump ring (Basics) and attach the bead unit's remaining loop. Close the jump ring.

6 Decide how long you want your necklace to be. Cut a 20–24-in. (51–61 cm) piece of suede lace. Cut the lace in half.

On each piece of lace, string a jump ring, leaving a 1-in. (2.5 cm) tail. Cut a 4-in. (10 cm) piece of 22-gauge wire. Wrap the wire ten times around the lace and tail. Use chainnose pliers to tuck the end of the wire under the wraps.

Copper connection

Mix a variety of beads for a long necklace and earthy earrings

by Carole Kane

Mismatched beads link to become an organic necklace of grand proportions. You can adjust the necklace by changing the length of the chain segments or the number of bead units. Take a hammer to copper hoops to give your earrings an equally organic texture.

Design alternative

For a more formal necklace, substitute pearl units for the gemstone units. If you use pearls, substitute 24-gauge wire for the 20-gauge wire.

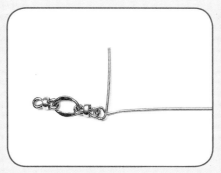

1 necklace • Cut 16 to 18 pieces of wire: three or four 3½-in. (8.9 cm) pieces, 11 5½-in. (14 cm) pieces, and two or three 6½-in. (16.5 cm) pieces. Cut 15 to 17 ¾-in. (1.9 cm) pieces of chain. On one end of each wire, make the first half of a wrapped loop (Basics, p. 12). Attach a chain and complete the wraps.

2 On one wire, string beads as desired. Make the first half of a wrapped loop. Repeat with the remaining wires.

3 Attach the unwrapped loop of one bead unit and the chain of another bead unit. Complete the wraps. Repeat until you've attached each bead unit. Attach the loop of the last bead unit to the end link of the first chain.

Supplies

Copper beads and findings from Riverstone Bead Company, riverstonebead.com.

necklace 44 in. (1.1 m)

- ◆ **2–4** 35–50 mm gemstones
- ◆ **4–6** 20–30 mm gemstones
- ◆ **2–4** 20–30 mm carved wood beads
- ◆ **3–6** 20–25 mm flat beads
- ◆ **25–40** 10–15 mm disk beads
- ◆ **15–30** 8–10 mm beads
- ◆ **5–12** 7 mm copper tube beads
- ◆ **35–60** 6 mm copper disk beads
- ◆ **30–45** 3–4 mm beads
- ◆ **8–12** 7 mm copper bead caps
- ◆ 7–8 ft. (2.1–2.4 m) 20-gauge half-hard copper wire
- ◆ 12–14 in. (30–36 cm) hammered long-and-short curb chain, 8 mm links
- ◆ chainnose and roundnose pliers
- ◆ diagonal wire cutters

earrings

- ◆ **2** 15 mm disk beads
- ◆ **4** 10 mm beads
- ◆ **4** 6 mm copper disk beads
- ◆ 10–15 in. (25–38 cm) 20-gauge half-hard copper wire
- ◆ pair of copper earring wires
- ◆ chainnose and roundnose pliers
- ◆ diagonal wire cutters
- ◆ bench block or anvil
- ◆ hammer

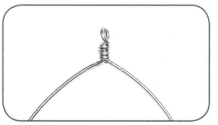

1 earrings • Cut a 5–7½-in. (13–19.1 cm) piece of wire. Wrap it around a cylindrical object to form a drop shape. String: 10 mm bead, copper disk bead, 15 mm disk bead, copper disk, 10 mm. Bend the wire upward ¾ in. (1.9 cm) from one end.

2 Make a set of wraps (Basics, p. 12). Make a wrapped loop (Basics) perpendicular to the drop.

3 On a bench block or anvil, hammer the wire to harden it. Turn the wire over and hammer the other side.

4 Open the loop of an earring wire (Basics). Attach the dangle and close the loop. Make a second earring to match the first.

by Diane Tadlock

Zen-inspired
necklace

Get reacquainted with your earthy side

When relaxing isn't an option, give the illusion of calm with an uncomplicated necklace and earrings. Wear this simple combination of wood, cinnabar, and leather as a plunging necklace, or trim the leather short for a choker.

1 necklace • On a head pin, string a 3 mm spacer and a pendant. Make a wrapped loop (Basics, p. 12). Cut a 16-in. (41 cm) piece of beading wire and center the pendant.

2 On each end, string: 6 mm spacer, wood bead, accent bead, bead cap, wood.

3 On each end, string: cinnabar bead, wood, 4 mm spacer, accent, wood, accent.

4 On each end, string a crimp bead and a triangular jump ring. Go back through the crimp bead, tighten the wire, and crimp the crimp bead (Basics). Trim the excess wire.

5 Decide how long you want your necklace to be and subtract the length of the beaded section. Double that measurement and cut two pieces of leather lace to that length. On each side, center the jump ring over the lace. Next to the jump ring, tie an overhand knot (Basics) with both ends.

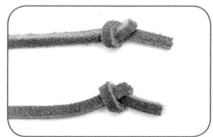

6 Check the fit and trim leather from each end if necessary. Tie an overhand knot at each end. To wear: Tie the ends into a bow.

1 earrings · On a head pin, string a spacer, a cinnabar bead, and a spacer. Make the first half of a wrapped loop (Basics, p. 12).

2 Attach the bead unit to a triangular jump ring and complete the wraps.

3 Open the loop of an earring wire (Basics) and attach the dangle. Close the loop. Make a second earring to match the first.

Supplies

necklace 16 in. (41 cm)
- 35–55 mm wood or cinnabar pendant
- **2** 20–26 mm cinnabar beads
- **8** 16 mm wood beads
- **6–8** 10–15 mm accent beads
- **2** 6 mm spacers
- **2** 4 mm spacers
- 3 mm spacer
- **2** 6 mm bead caps
- flexible beading wire, .014 or .015
- 35–45 in. (.89–1.1 m) leather lace, 2–3 mm wide
- 4-in. (10 cm) head pin
- **2** 8–10 mm triangular jump rings
- **2** crimp beads
- chainnose and roundnose pliers
- diagonal wire cutters
- crimping pliers (optional)

earrings
- **2** 20–26 mm cinnabar beads
- **4** 4 mm spacers
- **2** 2½-in. (6.4 cm) head pins
- **2** 8–10 mm triangular jump rings
- pair of earring wires
- chainnose and roundnose pliers
- diagonal wire cutters

" Working with color in designing jewelry has helped me as I pursue my degree in interior design. **"**

Tip

Many bead stores offer classes or studio areas where you can work on your latest beading project. Contact your local bead store to ask about class offerings.

Design alternative

As a dramatic alternative to traditional red, incorporate black cloisonné accent beads and black leather lace.

String it
with feeling

This texture-rich
necklace is as
pleasing to the touch
as it is to the eye

by Gretchen McHale

The smooth refinement of
pearls, the sharp precision
of crystals, and the
unpredictability of a trio
of novelty yarns make this
set feel as good as it looks.
Since the yarn takes center
stage in the necklace, give
the pearls their time to
shine in the earrings.

**"Look to everything around you for
inspiration and don't be afraid to try
new things."**

1 necklace • Decide how long you want your necklace to be. Add 8 in. (20 cm) and cut a piece of eyelash yarn to that length. Cut a piece of fuzzy yarn and two pieces of ribbon yarn to the same length. Cut a 36-in. (.9 m) piece of 24-gauge wire. Wrap the wire several times around all four strands 4 in. (10 cm) from one end.

2 On the wire, string a color A bicone crystal and a color B bicone and wrap the wire once around the strands. String a pearl and wrap the wire again. Repeat the pattern until the beaded section is the desired length. Every 3–4 in. (7.6–10 cm), wrap the wire several times around the yarn for stability. Make a set of wraps around all four strands 4 in. (10 cm) from the remaining end.

3 On a decorative head pin, string: color C bicone, flat spacer, pearl, spacer, color C bicone. Make the first half of a wrapped loop (Basics, p. 12). Make seven long bead units. Set one aside for step 8.

4 On a decorative head pin, string a pearl, a spacer, and a color A or B bicone. Make the first half of a wrapped loop. Make two short bead units.

5 Attach the bead units 1½ in. (3.8 cm) apart along the yarn strand, completing the wraps as you go. Attach the short bead units closer to the center, leaving 2 in. (5 cm) at the center of the strand for the pendant.

6 Cut a 10-in. (25 cm) piece of 20-gauge wire. Wrap over the end wraps of the 24-gauge wire. Make the first half of a wrapped loop. Attach half of a clasp and complete the wraps. Repeat on the other end.

7 Cut a 3-in. (7.6 cm) piece of 24-gauge wire. Make a wrapped loop on one end. String the bead pattern from step 3. Make a wrapped loop perpendicular to the first. Make two two-loop bead units.

8 Attach a long bead unit to a two-loop bead unit. Complete the wraps.

Open a 5 mm jump ring (Basics) and attach the remaining loop of the two-loop unit to the second two-loop unit. Close the jump ring. Use a 7 mm jump ring to attach the dangle and the loop of the clasp.

9 Use a 12 mm jump ring to attach a pendant to the center of the yarn strand.

1 earrings • On a decorative head pin, string a pearl, three color A bicone crystals, and one color B bicone. Make the first half of a wrapped loop (Basics, p. 12). Make two bead units. Following necklace step 3, make three long color B bead units. Following necklace step 4, make two short color A bead units.

2 Attach the bead units to an earring hoop as shown. Complete the wraps. Make a second earring to match the first.

Tip

If you are using a five-loop earring hoop, omit the smaller bead units.

Supplies

necklace 22 in. (56 cm)
- postage-stamp pendant (Eclectica, 262.641.0910)
- 16-in. (41 cm) strand 10 mm pearls
- **50–66** 4 mm bicone crystals, in three colors
- **18–26** 4 mm flat spacers
- 42 in. (1.1 m) 24-gauge half-hard wire
- 20 in. (51 cm) 20-gauge half-hard wire
- 28–32 in. (71–81 cm) eyelash yarn
- 28–32 in. (71–81 cm) fuzzy yarn
- 56–64 in. (1.4–1.6 m) ribbon yarn
- **9** 2-in. (5 cm) decorative head pins
- 12 mm jump ring
- 7 mm jump ring
- 5 mm jump ring
- toggle clasp
- chainnose and roundnose pliers
- diagonal wire cutters

earrings
- **14** 10 mm button pearls
- **32** 4 mm bicone crystals in two colors
- **16** 4 mm flat spacers
- **14** 2-in. (5 cm) decorative head pins
- pair of earring hoops with seven loops
- chainnose and roundnose pliers
- diagonal wire cutters

Design alternative

Sleeker yarns and earthy colors give the necklace a funky feel.

Recycled
by Jane Konkel
record albums and hemp twine

Get in the groove of stringing "green"

Before iPods, CDs, cassette tapes, or 8-tracks, there was vinyl. These groovy tree pendants are cut from recycled vinyl records, and the hemp twine is cultivated organically in western Romania. Hemp requires no herbicides, pesticides, or irrigation, and it improves soil quality as it grows, making recycled records and hemp an earth-friendly combination.

1 necklace • Decide how long you want your necklace to be. Triple that number and cut two pieces of twine to that length. Fold the pieces in half and string the ends through a pendant. Pull the ends through the resulting loop.

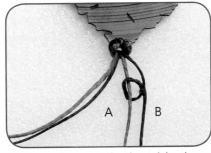

2 Place the pendant upside down at the top of your work surface and tie snake knots on one side of the pendant. To begin a snake knot: String piece B under and over piece A, making a loop.

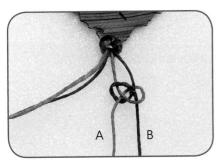

3 String A over B and through the first loop, making a loop with A. Pull both ends to loosely close the knot.

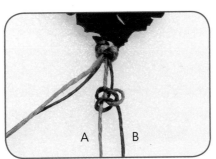

4 String B under A and down through A's loop. Pull B to loosely close the knot.

119

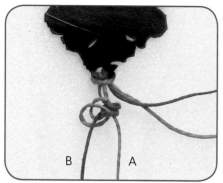

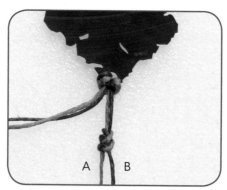

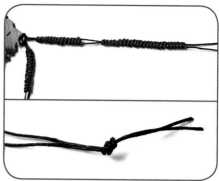

5 Turn the pieces over. String A under B and down through the lower of the two loops. Pull A to tighten the knot.

6 Turn the pieces over again, and repeat steps 4 and 5, tying snake knots to make a 1¼-in. (3.2 cm) knotted section on each side of the pendant.

7 Leave ½ in. (1.3 cm) of twine untied. Tie snake knots to make a 2½-in. (6.4 cm) knotted section. Check the fit, allowing for tying, and trim twine from each end if necessary. On each side, tie an overhand knot (Basics, p. 12) with both ends.

1 earrings • Open a jump ring (Basics, p. 12). Attach a pendant and another jump ring. Close the jump ring.

2 Open the loop of an earring thread (Basics) and attach the dangle. Close the loop. Make a second earring to match the first.

Supplies

Tree pendants from Alarm Industries, vlingvling.com. Hemp twine from Downbound, downbound.com.

necklace 18 in. (46 cm)
- 75 mm recycled-record pendant
- 8½–11½ ft. (2.6–3.5 m) waxed hemp twine
- diagonal wire cutters

earrings
- **2** 46 mm recycled-record pendants
- **4** 5 mm jump rings
- pair of earring threads
- chainnose and roundnose pliers

Tip

To keep my necklace simple, I omitted beads. Consider adding beads to your version. Limestone coral beads would be a "green" addition.

Adventures in color

by Stephanie A. White

Entwine strands of gemstones, pearls, and crystals in a multihued jewelry set

You'll love the combination of textures that comes together in these delicate, multidimensional pieces. Start with a mixed-color gemstone strand and add pearls and crystals. This necklace and bracelet both include tourmaline briolettes, but I chose muted colors for a dressy fall necklace and bright rondelles and crystals for a playful bracelet.

Tips

• For a budget-friendly option, try a strand of faceted glass rondelles in mixed colors

• In the necklace, I wanted the colors to balance on each side, so I started at the center. If stringing from one end to the other makes it easier to keep the wires taut, you can do that, too.

1 necklace • Decide how long you want your necklace to be, add 8 in. (20 cm), and cut two pieces of beading wire to that length. On one wire, center: bicone crystal, flat spacer, rondelle, flat spacer, bicone.

On the second wire, center: briolette, 3–4 mm pearl, 5–6 mm pearl, 3–4 mm pearl, briolette.

2 On each side, over both wires, string a round spacer. Separate the wires and continue stringing the patterns from step 1 on the same wire. Repeat until the necklace is within 1 in. (2.5 cm) of the finished length. (As you string, keep the wires taut so the briolette strand bows under the crystal strand.)

3 On each side, over both wires, string a round spacer, a crimp bead, a round spacer, and half of a clasp. Check the fit, and add or remove beads if necessary. Go back through the beads just strung and tighten the wires. Crimp the crimp bead (Basics, p. 12) and trim the excess wire. Use chainnose pliers to close a crimp cover over each finished crimp.

1 **bracelet** • On a head pin, string two or three beads as desired. Make the first half of a wrapped loop (Basics, p. 12). Set the bead unit aside for step 3.

Cut two 12-in. (30 cm) pieces of beading wire. Follow the patterns from steps 1 and 2 of the necklace until your bracelet within 1 in. (2.5 cm) of the desired length.

2 On one side, over both wires, string a round spacer, a crimp bead, a round spacer, and a lobster claw clasp. Repeat on the other end, substituting a 1-in. (2.5 cm) piece of chain for the clasp. Check the fit, and add or remove beads if necessary. Go back through the beads just strung and tighten the wires. Crimp the crimp beads (Basics) and trim the excess wire.

3 Attach the bead unit to the chain, and complete the wraps. Use chainnose pliers to close a crimp cover over each finished crimp.

Supplies

necklace 17 in. (43 cm)
- **23–27** 5–6 mm pearls, top drilled, in two colors
- **46–54** 3–4 mm pearls, top drilled, in two colors
- 15-in. (38 cm) strand 4–6 mm briolettes in assorted colors
- **23–27** 4–5 mm faceted rondelles
- **46–54** 4 mm bicone crystals in assorted colors
- **46–54** 3–4 mm flat spacers
- **26–30** 3 mm round spacers
- flexible beading wire, .010 or .012
- **2** crimp beads
- **2** crimp covers
- toggle clasp
- chainnose pliers
- diagonal wire cutters
- crimping pliers (optional)

bracelet
- **10–13** 5–6 mm pearls, top drilled, in two colors
- **20–26** 3–4 mm pearls, top drilled, in two colors
- **20–26** 4–6 mm briolettes left over from necklace

- **10–13** 4–5 mm faceted rondelles
- **20–26** 4 mm bicone crystals, in assorted colors
- **20–26** 3–4 mm flat spacers
- **13–16** 3 mm round spacers
- flexible beading wire, .010 or .012
- 1½-in. (3.8 cm) head pin
- **2** crimp beads
- **2** crimp covers
- lobster claw clasp
- 1 in. (2.5 cm) chain for extender, 4–5 mm links
- chainnose and roundnose pliers
- diagonal wire cutters
- crimping pliers (optional)

earrings
- **2** 4–5 mm faceted rondelles
- **2** 4 mm bicone crystals
- **2** 3–4 mm flat spacers
- **2** 2-in. (5 cm) jeweled head pins (Fire Mountain Gems, firemountain-gems.com)
- pair of earring wires
- chainnose and roundnose pliers
- diagonal wire cutters

1 **earrings** • On a jeweled head pin, string a rondelle, a spacer, and a bicone crystal. Make a plain loop (Basics, p. 12).

2 Open the loop of an earring wire (Basics) and attach the dangle. Close the loop. Make a second earring to match the first.

Necklace leaves a

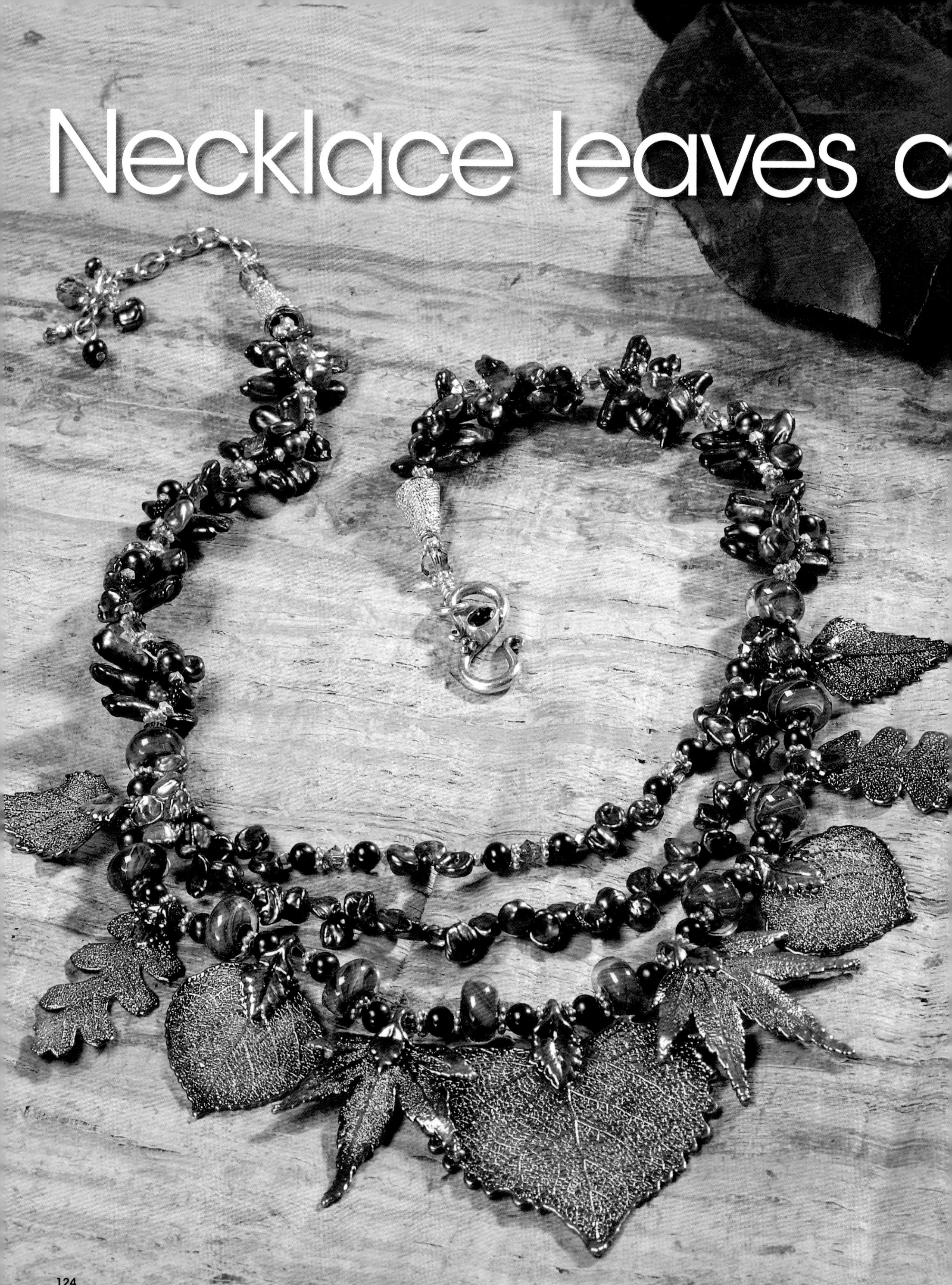

asting impression

Metallic flora sets the tone in this striking jewelry set

by Lisa Kan

Plan your design around these delicate leaves, choosing beads, pearls, and findings in coordinating colors and finishes. Use contrasting hues for a bolder statement, but keep the earrings subtle so your leafy look isn't overgrown.

1 necklace • Cut three pieces of beading wire (Basics, p. 12). On one wire, center: rondelle, flat spacer, round pearl, flat spacer, large leaf, bicone crystal, flat spacer, round pearl, flat spacer, rondelle. The pendant's loop should cover the bicone.

2 On each end, string: flat spacer, round pearl, flat spacer, bicone, small leaf, flat spacer, round pearl, flat spacer, rondelle. Repeat three times.

3 On the second wire, string petal pearls until the strand is 1 in. (2.5 cm) shorter than the beaded portion of the first strand. Center the pearls.

4 On the third wire, string: round pearl, flat spacer, bicone, flat spacer, round pearl, round spacer, three petal pearls. Repeat until the strand is 1 in. (2.5 cm) shorter than the beaded portion of the second strand, ending with a round pearl. Center the beads.

5 String each end of the second and third strands through the rondelles on each end of the first strand. On each side, over all three wires, string a flat spacer, a bicone, and a flat spacer.

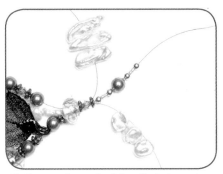

6 On each end of the first strand, string three stick pearls. On each end of the second strand, string: round spacer, two 11º seed beads, round spacer, round pearl, round spacer, two 11ºs, round spacer. On each end of the third strand, string three petal pearls.

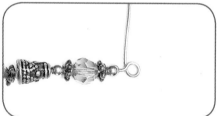

7a On each side, over all three strands, string a flat spacer, a bicone, and a flat spacer.

b Repeat steps 6 and 7a until the strands are within 2½ in. (6.4 cm) of the finished length. Check the fit, and add or remove beads from each end if necessary.

8 Cut two 3-in. (7.6 cm) pieces of 24-gauge wire. Make a wrapped loop on one end of each wire (Basics).

On each side, over all three strands, string: flat spacer, bicone, flat spacer, crimp bead, wrapped loop. Go back through the beads just strung. Tighten the wires and crimp the crimp bead (Basics).

9 On each end, string: cone, round spacer, flat spacer, round crystal, flat spacer, round spacer. Make the first half of a wrapped loop.

Supplies

necklace 20 in. (51 cm)
- **9** electroformed leaves, **1** 45–55 mm, **8** 30–45 mm
- **24–30** 16–18 mm stick pearls, center drilled
- 16-in. (41 cm) strand 6–8 mm petal pearls, top drilled
- **40–50** 4–6 mm round pearls
- **10** 10 mm lampworked rondelles
- **3** 6 mm round crystals
- **27–31** 4 mm bicone crystals

- 1 g 11º seed beads
- **68–76** 4 mm flat spacers
- **45–49** 3 mm round spacers
- flexible beading wire, .010 or .012
- 6 in. (15 cm) 24-gauge half-hard wire
- **5** 1½-in. (3.8 cm) head pins
- **2** crimp beads
- **2** cones
- S-hook or lobster claw clasp
- 2 in. (5 cm) cable chain for extender, 4–6 mm links
- chainnose and roundnose pliers
- diagonal wire cutters

- crimping pliers (optional)

earrings
- **2** 4–6 mm round pearls
- **4** 3 mm round spacers
- **2** 2-in. (5 cm) head pins
- **2** 4–5 mm jump rings
- **4** cones
- pair of lever-back earring wires
- chainnose and roundnose pliers
- diagonal wire cutters

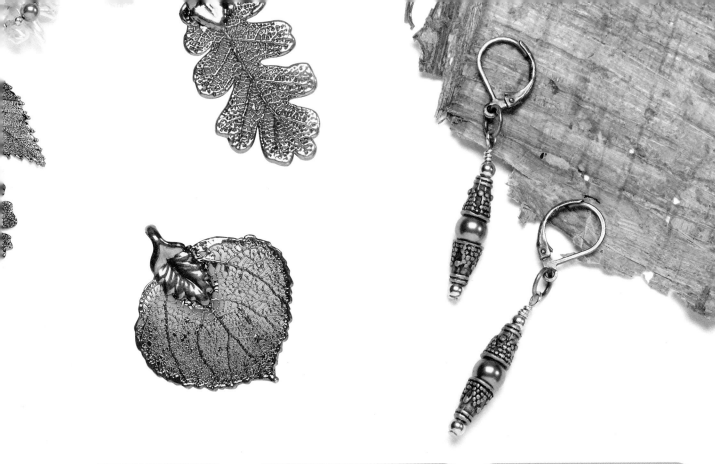

10 On one end, attach a clasp to a loop. Complete the wraps. Repeat on the other end, substituting a 2-in. (5 cm) piece of chain for the clasp.

11 On a head pin, string one or two beads and make the first half of a wrapped loop. Make five bead units. Attach the bead units to five links at the end of the chain. Complete the wraps.

Supply Notes

I used copper findings from Silver Enchantments, silverenchantments.com. My copper chain is from Ornamentea, ornamentea.com, and the other components are from Eclectica, (262) 641-0910. Leaves like these can be found at Rings & Things, rings-things.com.

1 earrings • On a head pin, string: round spacer, cone, round pearl, cone, round spacer. Make a wrapped loop (Basics, p. 12).

2 Open a jump ring (Basics). Attach the bead unit and the loop of an earring wire. Close the jump ring. Make a second earring to match the first.

Big beads,
no worries

Incorporate varied shapes and materials in an eye-catching necklace and earrings • by Marla Gulotta

I needed an accessory for a turtleneck sweater and decided it would be fun to make a longer necklace that had movement to it and was easy to wear. Because this necklace doesn't require a clasp, it looks good even if it shifts while I'm wearing it. Several pairs of earrings give me more options when I want to wear the set.

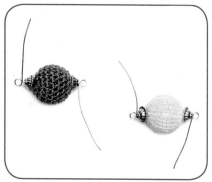

1 necklace • To make a round-bead unit: Cut a 4-in. (10 cm) piece of wire. Make the first half of a wrapped loop (Basics, p. 12). String a bead cap, a round bead, and a bead cap. Make the first half of a wrapped loop. Make seven round-bead units.

2 To make a disk unit: Follow step 1, substituting a 5–12 mm glass bead or crystal, a disk bead, and a 5–12 mm. Make two disk units.

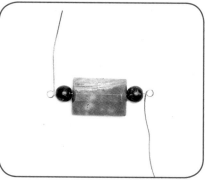

3 To make a flat-bead unit: Follow step 1, substituting a 5–12 mm, a flat bead, and a 5–12 mm. Make four flat-bead units.

66I so totally enjoy what I do that the only challenge is finding enough uninterrupted time to do all the projects that I keep envisioning.**99**

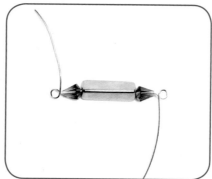

4 To make a tube-bead unit: Follow step 1, substituting a 5–12 mm, a tube-shaped bead, and a 5–12 mm. Make three tube-bead units.

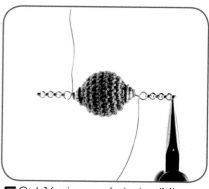

5 Cut 16 pieces of chain. (Mine are ½ in./1.3 cm each; cut 1-in./2.5 cm pieces for a longer necklace.) Attach a chain to each loop of one round-bead unit. Complete the wraps.

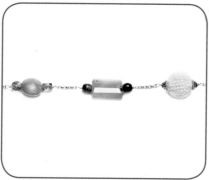

6 On each end, attach a loop of a disk unit. Attach: chain, flat-bead unit, chain, round-bead unit, chain. Complete the wraps as you go.

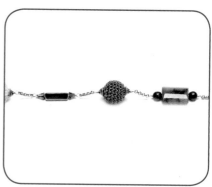

7 On each end, attach: tube-bead unit, chain, round-bead unit, chain, flat-bead unit, chain. Complete the wraps as you go.

8 On each end, attach a round-bead unit and a chain. Attach one loop of a tube-bead unit. Complete the wraps as you go.

1 earrings • On a head pin, string a bead cap, a round bead, and a bead cap. Make a plain loop (Basics, p. 12).

2 Cut a ½-in. (1.3 cm) piece of chain. Open the loop (Basics) of the bead unit and attach the chain. Close the loop. Open the loop of an earring post (Basics) and attach the dangle. Close the loop. Make a second earring to match the first.

Design alternatives

Create earrings that change the look of your jewelry when worn as a set. I made three options. First, I designed bubbly crocheted-bead earrings (p. 130–131). Then, I put together sleek, modern tube-bead earrings on longer chain. For an earthy accent, I added Hill Tribes silver earrings.

Supplies

necklace 33–35 in. (84–89 cm)
- ◆ **7** 18–22 mm round beads in two styles
- ◆ **4** 16–22 mm flat beads
- ◆ **3** 20 mm tube-shaped beads
- ◆ **2** 17–20 mm metal disk beads
- ◆ **18** 5–12 mm glass beads or crystals
- ◆ **14** 5–8 mm bead caps
- ◆ **64** in. (1.6 m) 20- or 22-gauge half-hard wire
- ◆ **10–18** in. (25–46 cm) chain, 4–5 mm links
- ◆ chainnose and roundnose pliers
- ◆ diagonal wire cutters

earrings
- ◆ **2** 18–22 mm round beads
- ◆ **4** 5–8 mm bead caps
- ◆ **1** in. (2.5 cm) chain, 4–5 mm links
- ◆ **2** 2-in. (5 cm) head pins
- ◆ pair of earring posts with ear nuts
- ◆ chainnose and roundnose pliers
- ◆ diagonal wire cutters

Tip

To cut many pieces of chain to the same length: Cut a piece to the desired length and string it on a needle or a head pin. String the longer chain and cut it to the length of the first piece. Repeat as necessary.

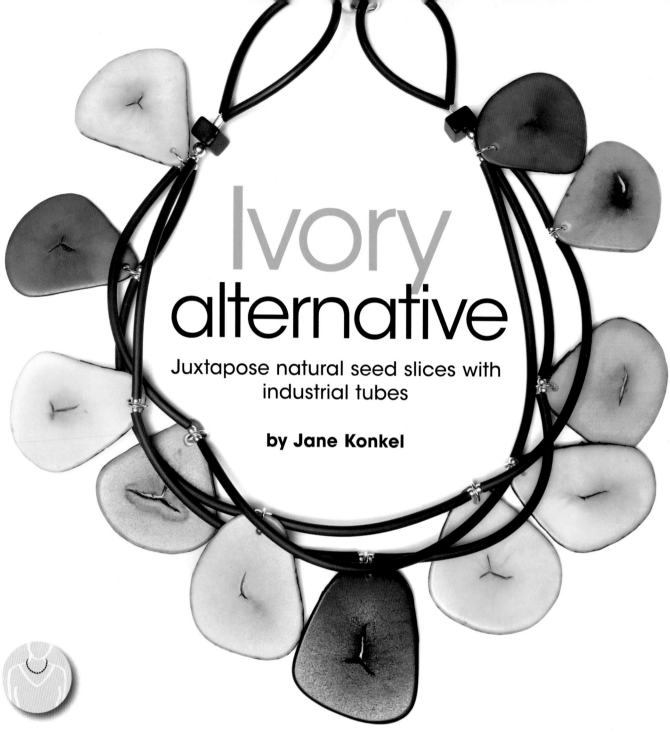

Ivory
alternative

Juxtapose natural seed slices with industrial tubes

by Jane Konkel

Tagua (*tah-gwa*) nuts grow on palm trees in the tropical rain forests of South America. After the pods ripen and fall to the ground, harvesters dry them. The seeds are separated from their shells, cut into different shapes, and then polished and dyed. Also called vegetable ivory, the natural color of tagua is white and resembles ivory from animals. Besides being a humane alternative to ivory, tagua products provide a sustainable income for indigenous people without harming trees.

Tip

For a slightly different version of this necklace, string rubber tubing on necklace-diameter memory wire. Use heavy-duty wire cutters to cut four coils.

1 Open a jump ring (Basics, p. 12) and attach a tagua slice. Close the jump ring. Repeat with the remaining tagua slices.

2 Cut three pieces of beading wire (Basics). On the first wire, center a 3 mm spacer, the black tagua unit, and a 3 mm spacer.

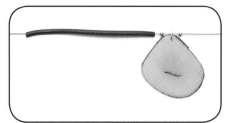

3 Cut two 3-in. (7.6 cm) pieces of rubber tubing. On each end of the first wire, string a 3-in. (7.6 cm) tube, a 3 mm spacer, a tagua unit, and a 3 mm spacer.

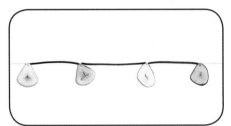

4 Cut one 2-in. (5 cm) and two 3-in. (7.6 cm) pieces of tubing. On the second wire, center the 2-in. (5 cm) tube.

5 On each end of the second wire, string a 3 mm spacer, a tagua unit, and a 3 mm spacer.

6 On each end of the second wire, string a 3-in. (7.6 cm) tube, a 3 mm spacer, a tagua unit, and a 3 mm spacer.

7 Cut one 4-in. (10 cm) and two 3-in. (7.6 cm) pieces of tubing. On the third wire, center the 4-in. (10 cm) tube.

On each end, string: 3 mm spacer, tagua unit, 3 mm spacer, 3-in. (7.6 cm) tube, 3 mm spacer, tagua unit, 3 mm spacer.

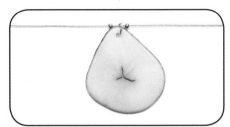

8 The beaded section of each strand should be within 4½ in. (11.4 cm) of the finished length. Cut tubing and string pieces on each end as necessary. On each end, string a tube and a 3 mm spacer.

9 On each end, over all three wires, string a 5 mm spacer, an irregular tagua bead, and a crimp bead.

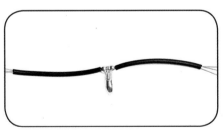

10 Cut one 4-in. (10 cm) and two 2-in. (5 cm) pieces of tubing. On one end, over all three wires, string: 2-in. (5 cm) tube, 5 mm spacer, lobster claw clasp, 5 mm spacer, 2-in. (5 cm) tube. On the other end, over all three wires, string the 4-in. (10 cm) tube.

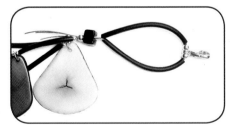

11 On each end, go back through the crimp bead, irregular tagua bead, and 5 mm spacer. Tighten the wires, crimp the crimp bead (Basics), and trim the excess wire.

Supplies

necklace 16 in. (41 cm)
- **11** 35–40 mm tagua slices, **1** black and **2** each in five colors (Acai-beads, acaibeads.com)
- **2** 6–9 mm irregular tagua beads (Acaibeads)
- **4** 5 mm large-hole spacers
- **26–28** 3 mm spacers
- flexible beading wire, .018 or .019
- 4–5 ft. (1.2–1.5 m) 2.5 mm rubber tubing
- **11** 5 mm jump rings
- **2** Mega crimp beads
- 16–20 mm lobster claw clasp
- chainnose and roundnose pliers, or **2** pairs of chainnose pliers
- Mighty Crimper crimping pliers
- diagonal wire cutters

Embracing a
natural
selection

Create a fall necklace that could be plucked from the forest floor • **by Eva Kapitany**

A finely veined leaf is a dramatic backdrop for a smaller electroformed pendant. Choose an acorn or four-leaf clover, a cypress or ginkgo leaf, a pinecone, or a maple pod. Coin pearls and faceted rondelles provide ethereal elegance to this otherwise earthy necklace.

1 On a head pin, string a 13º seed bead, a spacer, and a rondelle. Make the first half of a wrapped loop (Basics, p. 12). Repeat to make 19 or 20 rondelle units and four or five coin pearl units.

2 Cut a 2-in. (5 cm) piece of long-and-short–link chain. Attach three or four rondelle units and two or three pearl units to the chain. Complete the wraps as you go.

3 Complete the wraps on two rondelle units. Use a split ring (Basics) to attach a rondelle unit, the chain dangle, a rondelle unit, and a leaf pendant.

4 Decide how long you want your necklace to be. Cut a piece of cable chain to that length. On each end, attach a rondelle unit and a coin pearl unit.

5 Use a split ring to attach each end of the chain to the leaf pendant.

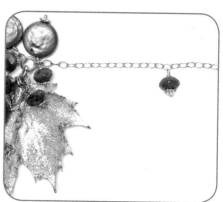

6 On one side, attach a rondelle unit 2 in. (5 cm) from the pendant. Continue attaching rondelle units, 2 in. (5 cm) apart, until you have attached six rondelle units. Repeat on the other side.

7 Open a jump ring (Basics) and attach the accent pendant to the leaf pendant. Close the jump ring.

Supplies

necklaces 33 in. (84 cm)
- **4–6** 45–55 mm filigree leaf pendant (Realm of the Goddess, realmofthegoddess.com)
- 30–40 mm accent pendant (Realm of the Goddess)
- **4 or 5** 10–14 mm coin pearls
- **19 or 20** 4–8 mm faceted gemstone rondelles
- **23–25** 13⁰ seed beads
- **23–25** 4 mm spacers
- 31–35 in. (79–89 cm) cable chain, 4–6 mm links
- 2 in. (5 cm) long-and-short-link chain
- **23–25** 1½-in. (3.8 cm) head pins
- 6 mm jump ring
- **2** 6 mm split rings
- chainnose, roundnose, and split-ring pliers
- diagonal wire cutters

Natural buttons and organic cotton yarn

by Naomi Fujimoto

To accent a bangle — if it's eco-friendly wood or shell, all the better — try buttons carved from bamboo, tagua nut, coconut, or sustainably harvested wood. Attach them with veggie-dyed or shade-grown yarn. Some of these undyed Peruvian cottons actually grow in hues of green, brown, or mauve without pesticides or chemicals.

Tie a green theme together

Supplies

Buttons and yarn available from Kusikuy, kusikuy.com, or Ecobutterfly, ecobutterfly.com.

- ♦ **4–8** 12–35 mm buttons
- ♦ **1–4** recycled-glass beads (optional)
- ♦ bangle bracelet with flat or beveled edge
- ♦ organic cotton yarn in different colors (see Tip, below)
- ♦ sewing needle or twisted-wire beading needle

1 Cut a 12–15-in. (30–38 cm) piece of yarn. Leaving a 2–3-in. (5–7.6 cm) tail, wrap the yarn around one section of a bangle, covering ½–1 in. (1.3–2.5 cm). Tie a surgeon's knot (Basics, p. 12). Do not trim the excess yarn yet.

2 Cut a 10–12-in. (25–30 cm) piece of yarn in a different color. Leaving a 2–3-in. (5–7.6 cm) tail, wrap the yarn around the covered section of the bangle as desired and tie a surgeon's knot.

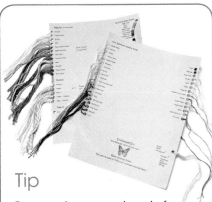

Tip

For yarns in an assortment of colors, order a sample card. I got mine from Ecobutterfly, ecobutterfly.com.

3 On a needle, string one end of the yarn from step 2. String a button or a glass bead and wrap the yarn around the bangle. Go through the button and around the bangle three or four times and tie a surgeon's knot.

4 Repeat steps 1–3 as desired. Trim the yarn ends as desired.

Glass

Hang on a
star

Turn an unlikely assortment of beads into a stellar constellation

by Jodi Broehm

For each of the five points of a Murano-style star pendant, string a strand with a different pattern of beads. Select a variety of beads in shades to highlight the star's foil accents. Wear your necklace rope-style by twisting the strands before putting it on.

1 necklace • Cut five pieces of beading wire (Basics, p. 12). On one wire, string seven to ten 11º seed beads. Center a pendant over the beads.

Supplies

necklace 16 in. (41 cm)
- 60 mm glass star pendant (GemMall.com)
- **8–12** 13 mm coin pearls
- **3–5** 9 mm faceted beads
- **8–12** 8–10 mm rondelles
- **21–25** 6 mm crystals
- 16-in. (41 cm) strand 6 mm pearls
- 16-in. (41 cm) strand 4 mm pearls
- 1 g 9º seed beads
- 5 g 11º seed beads
- 1 g 13º seed beads
- **2** 5 mm spacers
- flexible beading wire, .014 or .015
- 6 in. (15 cm) 20-gauge half-hard wire
- 1½-in. (3.8 cm) head pin
- **2** cones
- **10** crimp beads
- hook or S-hook clasp
- 2 in. (5 cm) chain for extender, 5–7 mm links
- chainnose and roundnose pliers
- diagonal wire cutters
- crimping pliers (optional)

earrings
- **2** 13 mm coin pearls
- **2** 9º seed beads
- **2** 11º seed beads
- **2** connectors with two loops
- **2** 2-in. (5 cm) decorative head pins
- pair of decorative earring wires
- chainnose and roundnose pliers
- diagonal wire cutters

2 On one side, string: 13º seed bead, crystal, 13º, seven 11ºs, 9º seed bead, 9 mm faceted bead, 9º, seven 11ºs, 13º, 6 mm pearl, 13º, seven 11ºs, 13º, coin pearl, 13º.

On the other side, string the pattern in reverse. Repeat the patterns on each side until the strand is within 3 in. (7.6 cm) of the finished length.

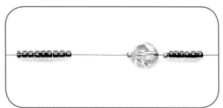

3 On the second wire, center the pendant over six to nine 11ºs (see Tip, below).

On each side of the pendant, string: 13º, crystal, 13º, six 11ºs. Repeat until the strand is within 3 in. (7.6 cm) of the finished length.

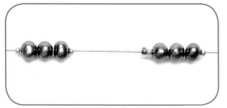

4 On the third wire, center the pendant over a 13º, three 4 mm pearls, and a 13º.

On each side, string an 11º, a 13º, three 4 mm pearls, and a 13º. Repeat until the strand is within 3 in. (7.6 cm) of the finished length.

Tip

To better show the patterns, steps 3 through 6 don't show the pendant over the first set of beads. On each strand, center your pendant over this first set of beads.

5 On the fourth wire, center the pendant over: two 11ºs, 13º, 4 mm pearl, 13º, 4 mm pearl, 13º, 4 mm pearl, 13º, two 11ºs.

On one side, string: 13º, coin, 13º, two 11ºs, 13º, 4 mm pearl, 13º, 4 mm pearl, 13º, 4 mm pearl, 13º, two 11ºs, 13º, crystal, 13º.

On the other side, string the pattern in reverse. Repeat the patterns on each side until the strand is within 3 in. (7.6 cm) of the finished length.

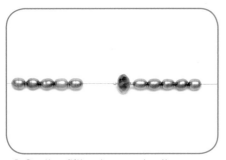

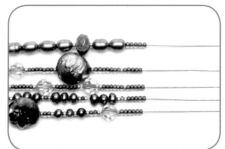

6 On the fifth wire, center the pendant over five 6 mm pearls.

On each side, string a 13º, a rondelle, a 13º, and five 6 mm pearls. Repeat until the strand is within 3 in. (7.6 cm) of the finished length.

7 On each end of each strand, string 11ºs until the strand is within 2½ in. (6.4 cm) of the finished length. Check the fit, allowing for finishing. Add or remove beads from each end if necessary.

8 Cut two 3-in. (7.6 cm) pieces of 20-gauge wire. On one end of each wire, make a wrapped loop (Basics).

On each end of each strand, string a crimp bead, an 11º, and a wrapped loop. Go back through the beads just strung, tighten the wire, and crimp the crimp bead (Basics).

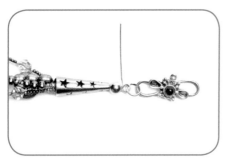

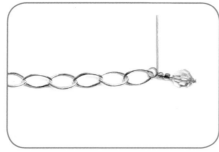

9 On each end, string a cone and a spacer. Make the first half of a wrapped loop.

On one end, attach a clasp and complete the wraps. Repeat on the other end, substituting a 2-in. (5 cm) chain for the clasp.

10 On a head pin, string a 13º, a crystal, a 13º, and two 11ºs. Make the first half of a wrapped loop. Attach the chain and complete the wraps.

"Sometimes when I'm feeling a design challenge, looking through past issues of *BeadStyle* magazine provides a solution.**"**

1 earrings • On a decorative head pin, string a coin pearl, a 9º seed bead, and an 11º seed bead. Make the first half of a wrapped loop (Basics, p. 12).

2 Attach a loop of a connector and complete the wraps.

3 Open the loop of an earring wire (Basics) and attach the dangle. Close the loop. Make a second earring to match the first.

Design alternative

Simplify your design by stringing just three strands. On each strand, string one type of bead alternating with seed beads.

European Union

String a luminous necklace and earrings with European glass

by Astrid Hall

Blown glass from Italy and cut glass from Austria form a beautiful alliance, as the precision of crystals contrasts with the soft, swirling colors within Venetian beads.

1 **necklace** • Cut a piece of beading wire (Basics, p. 12). Center a Venetian-glass focal bead on the wire.

2 On each end, string: rhinestone rondelle, 8º cylinder bead, round crystal, 8º, bead cap, Venetian accent bead, bead cap.

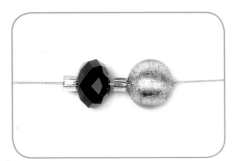

3 On each end, string an 8º, a crystal rondelle, an 8º, and a round Venetian bead. Repeat until the strand is within 1 in. (2.5 cm) of the finished length.

4 On each end, string a 6 mm round spacer, a crimp bead, and half of a clasp. Check the fit, and add or remove beads from each end if necessary. Go back through the last few beads strung and tighten the wire. Crimp the crimp bead (Basics) and trim the excess wire. The spacer may cover the finished crimp.

Supplies

The 14 mm round jet crystals are from Fusion Beads, fusionbeads.com. All other supplies are from Gems2Behold, gems2behold.com.

necklace 19 in. (48 cm)
- ◆ 25 x 40 mm oval Venetian-glass focal bead
- ◆ **2** 15 x 25 mm oval Venetian-glass accent beads
- ◆ **16–20** 8 mm round Venetian-glass beads
- ◆ **2** 14 mm round crystals
- ◆ **16–20** 8 mm crystal rondelles
- ◆ **2** 6 mm or 8 mm rhinestone rondelles
- ◆ 1 g 8º cylinder beads
- ◆ **2** 6 mm large-hole round spacers
- ◆ **4** 6 mm bead caps
- ◆ flexible beading wire, .018 or .019
- ◆ **2** crimp beads
- ◆ toggle clasp
- ◆ chainnose or crimping pliers
- ◆ diagonal wire cutters

earrings
- ◆ **2** 12 mm Venetian-glass beads
- ◆ **2** 8 mm crystal rondelles
- ◆ **2** 8 mm rhinestone rondelles
- ◆ **2** 8º cylinder beads
- ◆ **4** 6 mm bead caps or flat spacers
- ◆ **2** 2-in. (5 cm) head pins
- ◆ pair of earring wires
- ◆ chainnose and roundnose pliers
- ◆ diagonal wire cutters

1 earrings • On a head pin, string: bead cap or spacer, crystal rondelle, rhinestone rondelle, 12 mm Venetian-glass bead, bead cap or spacer, 8º cylinder bead. Make a wrapped loop (Basics, p. 12).

2 Open the loop of an earring wire (Basics). Attach the bead unit and close the loop. Make a second earring to match the first.

Design note

If you can't find 14 mm round crystals in the color you want, use 12 mm round crystals instead. They're available in a broader range of colors.

Real Venetian beads

string true

Spectacular beads go a long way when paired with distinctive chain

by Cathy Jakicic

There are any number of "Venetian-style" beads available. But just as no one would mistake the "Venice" built in a Las Vegas hotel for the romantic Italian city, imitation beads don't compare to authentic Italian glass beads, such as those made in Venice or Murano. Real Venetian beads can be made with 24k gold or .999 silver foil, gold leaf, or copper flakes. They are handcrafted by artisans, using secret glass recipes and traditional techniques passed down through generations.

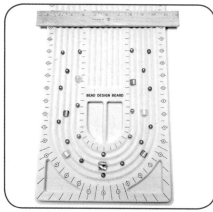

1 necklace • Decide how long you want your necklace strands to be. Mark the lengths on a bead design board and arrange Venetian beads in the channels.

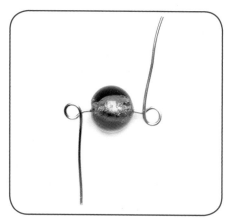

2 Cut a 2-in. (5 cm) piece of wire. Make the first half of a wrapped loop (Basics, p. 12). String a bead and make the first half of a wrapped loop. Put the bead unit back on the board. Repeat with the remaining beads.

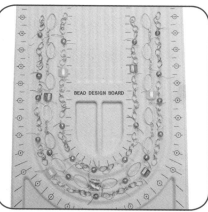

3 Measure the spaces between the bead units. Cut chain pieces to those lengths and position them on the board. Use cable chain for the longest and shortest strands. Use long-and-short–link chain for the middle strand.

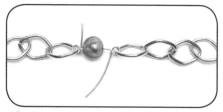

4 Attach the chains and bead units without completing the wraps. Check the fit, allowing 3 in. (7.6 cm) for finishing. Add or remove bead units or chain if necessary.

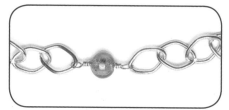

5 Complete the wraps on the bead units.

6 Trim one link from the cable chain to use as half of the clasp, and two 22 mm links from the long-and-short–link chain to use as jump rings.

Carefully cut the top of a 22 mm link and open it like a jump ring (Basics). Use it to attach one end of each strand and an S-hook clasp. Repeat on the other end, substituting the cable-chain link for the S-hook clasp.

Tip

Don't be afraid to mix and match beads made with different techniques. I used:
- 15 mm window flat square in amber and white
- 11 mm flat foil squares in amber
- 10 mm crystal matte cubes in amber
- 8 mm round foil beads in aqua and blue

1 **earrings** • On a head pin, string a Venetian bead. Make the first half of a wrapped loop (Basics, p. 12).

2 Cut a piece of chain with one long and three short links. Attach the bead unit to the long link. Complete the wraps.

3 Open the loop of an earring wire (Basics). Attach the dangle and close the loop. Make a second earring to match the first.

Design alternative

Saving your money for travel? Keep the necklace to one strand, being sure to use subtle but stunning blown-glass beads with a delicate, large-link chain.

Supplies

necklace (strands are 29 in./74 cm, 27 in./69 cm, and 26 in./66 cm)

- ◆ **25–29** assorted Venetian beads (Bella Venetian Beads, bellavenetianbeads.com)
- ◆ 50–60 in.(1.3–1.5 m) 22-gauge half-hard wire
- ◆ 38–46 in. (.97–1.2 m) cable chain, 12 mm links (Oriental Trading, orientaltrading.com)
- ◆ 20–24 in. (51–61 cm) long-and-short-link chain, 11 mm and 22 mm links (Oriental Trading)
- ◆ S-hook clasp
- ◆ chainnose and roundnose pliers
- ◆ diagonal wire cutters
- ◆ bead design board

earrings

- ◆ **2** 8 mm Venetian beads (Bella Venetian Beads, bellavenetianbeads.com)
- ◆ 4 in. (10 cm) long-and-short-link chain, 11 mm and 22 mm links (Oriental Trading, orientaltrading.com)
- ◆ **2** 1½-in. (3.8 cm) head pins
- ◆ pair of earring wires
- ◆ chainnose and roundnose pliers
- ◆ diagonal wire cutters

"Venice is my favorite city. For me, the beads that are made there seem to glow with the city's magic."

Blue ribbon style

This necklace and earrings pair fabric with glass beads

by Ute Bernsen

Go with the flow of silk ribbons, balancing symmetry with casually placed knots to create richly colored waves accented by the sparkle of dichroic-glass beads.

1 **necklace** · Center a large bead over all five ribbons.

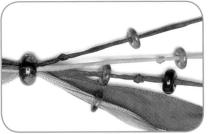

2 On each side, tie overhand knots (Basics, p. 12) on three to five ribbons. String five small beads as shown.

3 On each end, string a large bead over all five ribbons approximately 4 in. (10 cm) from the center bead. Repeat step 2.

4 On each side, over all five ribbons, string a large bead 7 in. (18 cm) from the last bead strung. Decide how long you want your necklace to be. On each side, over all five ribbons, string half of a clasp, positioning it to create the desired length.

5 On each side, string a small bead on the three thinnest strands. Tie an overhand knot next to each bead.

Tips

Blue-green necklace
• Dichroic-glass beads from Paula Radke, paularadke.com.
Blue-violet necklace
• Borosilicate glass beads by Jenny E. from Jah-Love's Creations, jahluv420@earthlink.net, seemyglass.com.
• Recycled-glass beads from Bead to Feed, beadtofeed.org.

Supplies

necklace 24 in. (61 cm)
- 30–32 8–15 mm large-hole beads
- Beautiful Silk ribbon mix (Silk Painting is Fun, silkpaintingisfun.com)
- hook clasp with large loops

earrings
- 8 8 mm large-hole beads
- 16 in. (41 cm) silk string, 2 mm diameter (Silk Painting is Fun, silkpaintingisfun.com)
- pair of earring wires
- chainnose and roundnose pliers, or 2 pairs of chainnose pliers

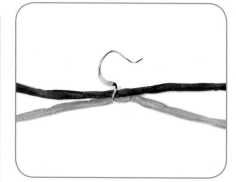

1 **earrings** • Cut two 4-in. (10 cm) pieces of silk string. Open the loop of an earring wire (Basics, p. 12). Center the loop over both strings. Close the loop.

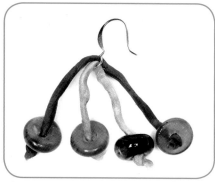

2 String a bead on each end. Tie an overhand knot (Basics) next to each bead. Make a second earring to match the first.

Design alternative

Use gold and silver ribbons and beads to create a dressy accent.

66Get out of your comfort zone and do something new. When I think outside the box, I create the most wonderful jewelry.**99**

Learn an easy
crisscross technique

by Betty E. Rodriguez

Weave a lush necklace

Although putting together this swag-style necklace may seem daunting, it's actually a cinch. A basic crisscross weave creates an intertwined look. For a necklace resembling a thick, textured vine, use this technique with top-drilled beads. A pendant spilling from the necklace makes this piece truly luscious.

1 On a head pin, string a 3–5 mm bead. Make the first half of a wrapped loop (Basics, p. 12). Repeat to make a total of eight 3–5 mm (small) bead units, eight 6–9 mm (medium) bead units, eight 10–12 mm (large) bead units, and eight 11 mm leaf units.

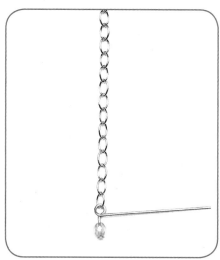

2 Cut a 2¼-in. (5.7 cm) piece of chain. Attach a small-bead unit to the bottom link and complete the wraps.

3 Skip a few links and attach small-bead units, then medium-bead units, and then large-bead units, to the remaining links, completing the wraps as you go. Attach the eight leaf units to the top links of the chain, as shown.

4 Open a jump ring (Basics). Attach the loop half of a toggle clasp to the top chain link. Close the jump ring. Set the pendant aside for step 7.

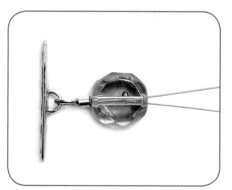

5 Decide how long you want your necklace to be. Triple that measurement and cut a piece of beading wire to that length. Center the bar half of the toggle clasp on the wire.

Over both ends of the wire, string a crimp bead and a 10 mm bead. Flatten the crimp bead (Basics).

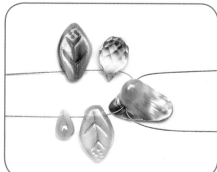

6 On each end, string two top-drilled beads. On one end, string a blister pearl or a 14 mm leaf bead. Pass the other end through the bead in the opposite direction. Tighten the wires, sliding the fifth bead toward the first four and making sure it stays upright.

Repeat, varying the top-drilled beads strung, until the strand is within 1 in. (2.5 cm) of the finished length.

How many beads are in a strand?

bead size	average number of beads per 16-in. (41 cm) strand	beads are shown actual size
3 mm	136	
4 mm	102	
5 mm	81	
6 mm	68	
8 mm	50	
10 mm	41	
12 mm	34	
14 mm	29	
16 mm	25	

Briolettes are often sold in strands strung with separators, so the number of briolettes in a 16-in. (41 cm) strand will be fewer than in a strand with only beads.

Chart data from Shipwreck Beads

7 Over both ends, string a 10 mm bead, a crimp bead, and the loop of the pendant. Check the fit, and add or remove beads if necessary. Go back through the beads just strung, tighten the wires, and flatten the crimp bead. Trim the excess wire. If desired, use chainnose pliers to close a crimp cover over each finished crimp.

Supplies

necklace 16 in. (41 cm)

◆ **2** 16-in. (41 cm) strands 10–28 mm blister pearls, top drilled
◆ **160-200** 7–16 mm beads, top drilled, in six to eight shapes
◆ **8-12** 14 mm leaf beads, top drilled
◆ **24** 3–12 mm beads, in assorted shapes
◆ **8** 11 mm leaf beads
◆ **2** 10 mm crystals
◆ flexible beading wire, .010 or .012
◆ 2¼ in. (5.7 cm) chain, 2–3 mm links
◆ **32** 2-in. (5 cm) head pins
◆ 10 mm jump ring
◆ **2** crimp beads
◆ **2** crimp covers (optional)
◆ toggle clasp
◆ chainnose and roundnose pliers
◆ diagonal wire cutters

Chinese lanterns

Light up the night with a pair of festive earrings

by Sue Kennedy

The Lantern Festival is a traditional Chinese festival celebrated on the 15th day of the Chinese New Year. During the full moon, thousands of colorful lanterns are hung. But there's no need to wait for a full moon or even a special occasion — you can make these earrings in a matter of minutes and wear them tonight.

1 On a decorative head pin, string a crystal and make a plain loop (Basics, p. 12). Make three crystal units.

2 Cut a 2½-in. (6.4 cm) piece of wire and make a wrapped loop (Basics). String a rondelle, a lampworked bead, and a rondelle. Make a wrapped loop.

3 Open the loop (Basics) of a crystal unit and attach a loop of the bead unit. Close the loop. Repeat with the remaining crystal units.

"I hope my beads put a smile on the faces of the people who buy them."

4 Open the loop of an earring wire and attach the dangle. Close the loop. Make a second earring to match the first.

Design alternative

Try lampworked beads in another shape, or string crystals in different colors.

Supplies

- 2 16 mm lampworked beads (SueBeads, suebeads.com,)
- 4 6 mm rondelles
- 6 4 mm crystals
- 2 9º seed beads (optional)
- 5 in. (13 cm) 24-gauge half-hard wire
- 6 1½-in. (3.8 cm) decorative head pins
- pair of earring wires
- chainnose and roundnose pliers
- diagonal wire cutters

Tip

To embellish earring wires, dot glue on each wire above the loop and string a seed bead.

Fusilli bracelet

This bracelet recipe mixes curly tubes with lampworked beads

by Alice Lauber

Shaped like fusilli pasta, these curly silver tube beads make a satisfying complement to striking art beads. For a palette-pleasing bracelet-and-earring set, string brilliant blue lampworked beads and season with a mix of crystals.

1 bracelet • Cut a piece of beading wire (Basics, p. 12). Center a crystal, a 10 mm lampworked bead, and a spacer.

2 On each end, string a curly tube bead, a crystal, a 10 mm, and a crystal.

3 On each end, string a curly tube, a crystal, and a 10 mm. On one end, string a crystal; on the other end, string a spacer.

4 On each end, string a crimp bead, a crystal, and half of a clasp. Check the fit, and add or remove beads if necessary. Go back through the beads just strung and tighten the wire. Crimp the crimp bead (Basics) and trim the excess wire.

1 earrings • On a decorative head pin, string a spacer, a 10 mm lampworked bead, a spacer, and a crystal. Make a wrapped loop (Basics, p. 12).

2 Open the loop of an earring wire (Basics). Attach the dangle and close the loop. Make a second earring to match the first.

Recycled-glass
buttons

Make a bracelet and earring set with simple shapes

by Jane Konkel

As a child, Nomoda Ebenizer Djaba, also called "Cedi," worked with his grandfather in their family bead-making business. Today Cedi is the director and owner of the Retado Bead Industry in Odumasi Krobo, Ghana. The workshop has several employees who crush glass from bottles or broken window panes, funnel it into clay molds, and fire it in a wood-burning kiln. Visit Cross Cultural Collaborative, Inc. at culturalcollaborative.org to see a video of this bead-making process.

1 bracelet • Open one of the bracelet's jump rings (Basics, p. 12) and remove a disk. Close the jump ring. Remove every other disk, so you have five to seven disk units with two attached jump rings.

2 Use two 9 mm jump rings to attach two disk units. Use pairs of jump rings to attach the remaining disk units until the bracelet is within 1 in. (2.5 cm) of the finished length.

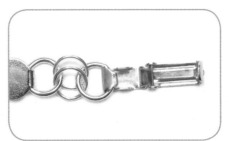

3 On one end, use a pair of 9 mm jump rings to reattach the clasp. When closed, the front of the clasp should be visible.

4 Dot a disk with glue and apply a button. Repeat with the remaining buttons.

Tip

The disk-and-loop chain for this bracelet is available as preassembled bracelets or in 32-ft. (9.7 m) spools. If you opt for the spools, don't forget the fold-over clasps.

1 earrings • Open a 9 mm jump ring (Basics, p. 12). Attach a loop of a disk. Close the jump ring.

2 Use two 9 mm jump rings to attach the disk unit and another 9 mm jump ring.

3 Dot the disk with glue and apply a button.

4 Open the loop of an earring wire (Basics) and attach the dangle. Close the loop. Make a second earring to match the first.

Supplies

bracelet
- ◆ **5–7** 12–24 mm recycled-glass buttons (africancraft.com/shop; go to "Aba's shop")
- ◆ disk-and-loop bracelet (Rings & Things, rings-things.com)
- ◆ **10–14** 9 mm jump rings
- ◆ chainnose and roundnose pliers, or **2** pairs of chainnose pliers
- ◆ Super New Glue adhesive (Rings & Things)

earrings
- ◆ **2** 12–24 mm recycled-glass buttons (africancraft.com/shop; go to "Aba's shop")
- ◆ **2** disks left over from bracelet
- ◆ **8** 9 mm jump rings
- ◆ pair of earring wires
- ◆ chainnose and roundnose pliers, or **2** pairs of chainnose pliers
- ◆ Super New Glue adhesive (Rings & Things, rings-things.com)

Eco-friendly recycled glass

String a stylish set with good conscience

by Cathy Jakicic

These beads are made from recycled glass bottles and come in a variety of colors. The beads resemble sea glass found on a beach, but are much easier to find!

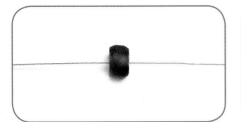

1 **necklace** • Cut three pieces of beading wire (Basics, p. 12), each 2 in. (5 cm) longer than the previous piece. On the shortest wire, center a rondelle.

2 On each end, string 1½ in. (3.8 cm) of chips and a rondelle. Repeat twice.

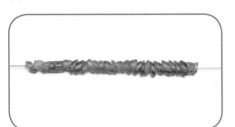

3 On the middle wire, center 3 in. (7.6 cm) of chips.

4 On each end, string a rondelle, a chip, a rondelle, and 3 in. (7.6 cm) of chips. Repeat.

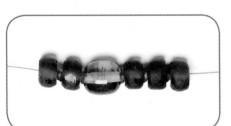

5 On the longest wire, center: rondelle, chip, rondelle, chip, round bead, chip, rondelle, chip, rondelle, chip, rondelle.

6 On each end, string: 2¾ in. (7 cm) of chips, rondelle, chip, rondelle, chip, rondelle. Repeat twice.

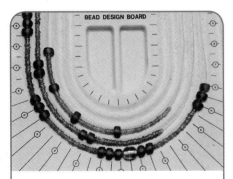

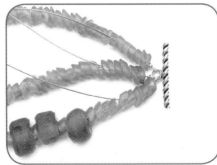

7 On each end of each strand, string chips until the strands are within 1 in. (2.5 cm) of the finished length.

On each end of each strand, string a crimp bead and half of a clasp. Check the fit, and add or remove beads if necessary. Go back through the last few beads strung and tighten the wire. Crimp the crimp bead (Basics) and trim the excess wire.

Tips

• Arrange your strands on a bead design board as you string to make sure the rondelles are properly spaced.

• Skip the 18 mm round bead and add more rondelles if you don't want to buy a whole strand for just one bead. Or make a second beautiful necklace with the rest of the 18 mm beads!

Supplies

Recycled-glass beads from Happy Mango Beads, happymangobeads.com.

necklace 18–22 in. (46–56 cm)
◆ 18 mm recycled-glass round bead
◆ 16-in. (41 cm) strand 12 mm recycled-glass rondelles
◆ **2** 24-in. (61 cm) strands 5 mm recycled-glass chips
◆ flexible beading wire, .018 or .019
◆ **6** crimp beads
◆ toggle clasp
◆ chainnose or crimping pliers
◆ diagonal wire cutters

earrings
◆ **8** 5 mm recycled-glass chips
◆ **8** 2-in. (5 cm) head pins
◆ pair of lever-back earring wires
◆ chainnose and roundnose pliers
◆ diagonal wire cutters

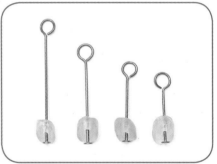

1 **earrings** • On a head pin, string a chip. At the end of the head pin, make a plain loop (Basics, p. 12). Cut a head pin slightly shorter than the previous one and make a chip unit. Make two more chip units in the same way.

2 Open the loop of an earring wire (Basics). Attach the chip units and close the loop. Make a second earring to match the first.

Ahead of the curve

This smart set goes from dressy to casual by playing it by ear-rings

by Melissa Rediger

A simple design draws attention right where it should be — front and center. The swirling colors of a crescent lampworked bead stand out against solid-colored, twisted wood beads. Pair your necklace with wood earrings for daywear, or don the lampworked earrings for more formal attire.

1 necklace • Cut a piece of beading wire (Basics, p. 12). On the wire, string: wood bead, 11 mm spacer, curved bead, 11 mm, wood. Center the beads on the wire.

2 On each end, string: 5 mm spacer, wood, 5 mm spacer, accent bead, 5 mm spacer. Repeat.

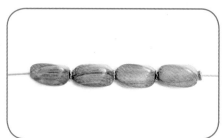

3 On each end, string a wood bead and a 5 mm spacer, repeating until the strand is within 1 in. (2.5 cm) of the finished length.

4 On each end, string a crimp bead, a 5 mm spacer, and half of a clasp. Check the fit, and add or remove beads from each end if necessary. Go back through the last few beads strung and tighten the wire. Crimp the crimp bead (Basics) and trim the excess wire.

Supplies

necklace 15½ in. (39.4 cm)

- 52 mm curved lampworked bead (Sea of Glass, mjrbeads.com)
- 16-in. (41 cm) strand 15 mm twisted wood bead (Beads and Pieces, beadsandpieces.com)
- **4** 10–14 mm accent beads
- **2** 11 mm spacers
- **20–26** 5 mm spacers
- flexible beading wire, .014 or .015
- **2** crimp beads
- toggle clasp
- chainnose or crimping pliers
- diagonal wire cutters

wood-bead earrings

- **2** 15 mm twisted wood beads (Beads and Pieces, beadsandpieces.com)

- **4** 5 mm spacers
- **2** 2-in. (5 cm) head pins
- pair of earring wires
- chainnose and roundnose pliers
- diagonal wire cutters

lampworked-bead earrings

- **2** 15 mm lampworked beads (Sea of Glass, mjrbeads.com)
- **4** 4–5 mm crystals, in two colors
- **2** 5 mm flat spacers
- **2** 3 mm round spacers
- **2** 2-in. (5 cm) head pins
- pair of decorative lever-back earring wires
- chainnose and roundnose pliers
- diagonal wire cutters

1 wood-bead earrings • On a head pin, string a spacer, a wood bead, and a spacer. Make a wrapped loop (Basics, p. 12).

2 Open the loop of an earring wire (Basics) and attach the dangle. Close the loop. Make a second earring to match the first.

1 lampworked-bead earrings • On a head pin, string: 3 mm spacer, lampworked bead, crystal, 5 mm spacer, crystal in a second color. Make a wrapped loop (Basics, p. 12).

2 Open the loop of an earring wire (Basics) and attach the dangle. Close the loop. Make a second earring to match the first.

Easy way around

Simply wrapped flexible beading wire lets you string "hole-less" beads

by Alice Lauber

Nestle circles of seed beads in the ridge of glass yo-yo beads to create a clever bracelet-and-earring set. Because seed beads and crystals come in virtually every color under the sun, you can play with mixing different shades of blue — or create drama with contrasting colors.

Supplies

bracelet
- **7-9** 11 mm yo-yo beads (Midwest Beads, midwestbeads.biz)
- **4-6** 8 mm crystal rondelles
- **4-6** 8 mm bicone crystals
- 2 g 11º seed beads
- flexible beading wire, .010 or .012
- **2** crimp beads
- lobster claw clasp
- 6 mm split ring
- chainnose or crimping pliers
- diagonal wire cutters

earrings
- **2** 11 mm yo-yo beads (Midwest Beads, midwestbeads.biz)
- **4** 8 mm bicone crystals
- **60-64** 11º seed beads
- flexible beading wire, .010 or .012
- **2** crimp beads
- pair of earring wires
- chainnose or crimping pliers
- diagonal wire cutters

1 bracelet • Decide how long you want your bracelet to be. Double that length, add 6 in. (15 cm), and cut two pieces of beading wire to that length. About 3 in. (7.6 cm) from one end, over both wires, string an 11º seed bead, a rondelle, and an 11º.

2 On each wire, string 11 11ºs.

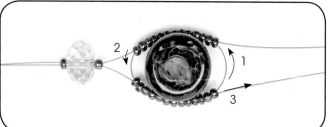

3 Position a yo-yo bead between the wires, and make sure there are enough 11ºs to encircle it. String one wire back through the 11ºs on both wires.

4a Over both wires, string an 11º, a bicone crystal, and an 11º. Tighten the wires around the yo-yo.

b Repeat steps 2–4a until the bracelet is within 1 in. (2.5 cm) of the finished length, alternating rondelles and bicones in step 4a. Also, alternate the wire end that encircles the yo-yos.

5 Check the fit, allowing 1 in. (2.5 cm) for finishing, and add or remove beads if necessary. On one side, over both wires, string a crimp bead, an 11º, and a lobster claw clasp. Go back through the beads just strung and tighten the wires. Repeat on the other side, substituting a split ring for the clasp. Crimp the crimp beads (Basics, p. 12) and trim the excess wire.

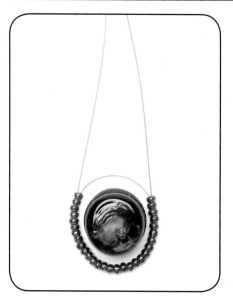

1 earrings • Cut a 5-in. (13 cm) piece of beading wire. String 29 11º seed beads on the wire. String one wire end back through all of the 11ºs. Position a yo-yo bead within the 11ºs.

2 Over both ends, string an 11º, a bicone crystal, a crimp bead, and a bicone. Tighten the wire around the yo-yo.

3 Over both ends, string the loop of an earring wire and go back through the last three beads strung. Tighten the wire. Crimp the crimp bead (Basics, p. 12) and trim the excess wire. Make a second earring to match the first.

Loopy for color

Cluster teardrop beads in a sweet ring

by Jessica Fehrman

This simple wirework ring boasts a burst of color that can be as orderly or free-form as you feel. Carefully arrange the teardrop beads with your fingers after each wire loop, or let them fall where they may.

1 Cut a 16-in. (41 cm) piece of wire. String a teardrop bead and the loop of a ring base. Make a set of wraps (Basics, p. 12) under the loop. Trim the excess wire from the wraps.

2 Continue stringing teardrops and wrap the wire through the ring's loop after each bead. Pull the wire tight after each wrap.

3 When it's no longer possible to wrap the wire through the ring's loop, weave the wire back and forth through previous wire wraps after stringing each additional teardrop. To finish, bring the wire to the base of the ring loop and wrap the wire snugly around the loop. Trim the excess wire.

Tip

To tighten up the wire loops once the beads are strung, use chainnose pliers to twist the looser wires as close to the base as possible.

Supplies

- ◆ **14–20** 6 mm glass teardrop beads
- ◆ 14–18 in. (36–46 cm) 26-gauge half-hard wire
- ◆ ring base with one loop
- ◆ chainnose pliers
- ◆ diagonal wire cutters

Coiled wire and lampworked beads unite in a bracelet

by Carolyn Conley

Razzle-dazzle
bracelet

The first time I laid eyes on lampworked beads, I was captivated by their beauty. So, using a book and video, I taught myself to make them. After many long days, burned fingers, and misshapen beads, I finally was able to create my own. After Hurricane Katrina hit the Gulf Coast in 2005, I incorporated my lampworked beads into coiled-wire bracelets like the ones shown here. I auctioned them on eBay and donated the proceeds to the Red Cross for hurricane relief.

Supplies

- **3** 19–20 mm lampworked lentil beads (CC Design, beadsbyccdesign.com)
- **10–14** 6 mm crystals
- **6–10** 3 mm spacers
- flexible beading wire, .018 or .019
- 12 ft. (3.7 m) 22-gauge dead-soft wire
- 14 in. (36 cm) 18-gauge half-hard wire
- **8** 1½-in. (3.8 cm) head pins
- **8** 11 mm twisted jump rings (Java Bead, javabead.com)
- **2** crimp beads
- toggle clasp
- chainnose and roundnose pliers
- diagonal wire cutters
- Coiling Gizmo with 3 mm diameter rod (coilinggizmo.com) or Twist 'n' Curl with 2 mm diameter rod (twistncurl.com)
- crimping pliers (optional)

Tip

Adjust the length of the beaded section of your bracelet by adding or removing crystals and spacers in step 7. You can also adjust the length of the coiled section slightly by gently pushing together or pulling apart the coils.

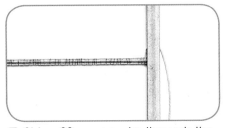

1 String 22-gauge wire through the handle of a coiling tool and bend one end to anchor it. Turn the handle to wrap the wire until the coiled wire is 10 in. (25 cm).

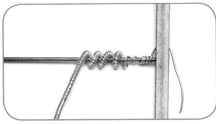

2 Remove the coiled wire and center it on a 14-in. (36 cm) piece of 18-gauge wire. Anchor the 18-gauge wire through the handle. Turn the handle three or four times to wrap the wire. Keeping the coil against the last wrap, continue to wrap the entire coil.

3 Remove the coil. On each end of the 18-gauge wire, string a jump ring and make the first half of a wrapped loop (Basics, p. 12).

4 On a head pin, string a crystal and make a wrapped loop. Make eight bead units.

5 On one loop, attach two bead units, the loop half of a toggle clasp, and two bead units. Complete the wraps. Attach four bead units on the other loop and complete the wraps.

6 Cut a 9-in. (23 cm) piece of beading wire. String: crystal, spacer, jump ring, lampworked bead, jump ring, spacer, crystal. Center the beads.

7 On each end, string: spacer, jump ring, lampworked bead, spacer, jump ring, crystal.

8 On one end, string a crimp bead and the coiled section's loop. On the other end, string a crimp bead and the bar half of the clasp. Check the fit, and add or remove beads if necessary.

9 Go back through the last few beads strung and tighten the wire. Crimp the crimp beads (Basics) and trim the excess wire.

Bead to Feed

These strands support a noteworthy cause

by Cathy Jakicic

The Nyame Adom Foundation of America is building a series of small orphanages to help children orphaned by the AIDS epidemic in Ghana. NAFofA's mission is to teach the children how to become self-reliant. One of NAFofA's fund-raising avenues is the Bead to Feed program. Recycled-glass beads made by Ghanian artisans are purchased by NAFofA and resold. NAFofA says 100 percent of the proceeds from the bead sales go to support the orphanages. For more information, visit nafofa.org or beadtofeed.org.

Tip

One strand of the recycled-glass rondelles is enough for the necklace and earrings, but getting two strands in different shades of blue makes the pattern more interesting. And you know the extra expense is supporting a good cause!

1 **a necklace** • Cut two pieces of beading wire, one 4 in. (10 cm) longer than the other (Basics, p. 12).
b On the short wire, center: spacer, pearl, round recycled-glass bead, pearl, spacer.

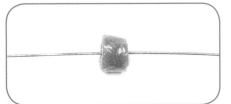

2 **a** On each end, string a recycled-glass tube bead.
b On each end, repeat the patterns in steps 1b and 2a until the strand is within 1½ in. (3.8 cm) of the finished length.

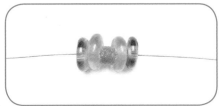

3 On the long wire, center two recycled-glass rondelles, a tube, and two rondelles.

4 On each end, string: spacer, two rondelles, tube, two rondelles, spacer.

5 **a** On each end, string a pearl, a round bead, a pearl, and a spacer.
b On each end, repeat the patterns in steps 3, 4, and 5a until the strand is within 2 in. (5 cm) of the finished length.

6 On each end of the short strand, string four spacers, a crimp bead, a spacer, and half of a clasp.

On each end of the long strand, string three spacers, a crimp bead, a spacer, and half of the clasp.

Check the fit, and add or remove beads if necessary. Go back through the beads just strung and tighten the wires. Crimp the crimp beads (Basics) and trim the excess wire.

Supplies

necklace 20½ in. (52.1 cm)
- 16-in. (41 cm) strand 12 mm round recycled-glass beads
- 16-in. (41 cm) strand 10 mm recycled-glass rondelles
- 16-in. (41 cm) strand 6 mm recycled-glass tube beads
- **38–44** 6 mm round pearls
- **66–80** 3 mm round spacers
- flexible beading wire, .014 or .015
- 4 crimp beads
- toggle clasp
- chainnose or crimping pliers
- diagonal wire cutters

earrings
- **4** 10 mm recycled-glass rondelles
- **4** 6 mm round pearls
- **2** 3 mm round spacers
- **2** 2-in. (5 cm) head pins
- pair of earring wires
- chainnose and roundnose pliers
- diagonal wire cutters

1 **earrings** • On a head pin, string a spacer, a pearl, two recycled-glass rondelles, and a pearl. Make a wrapped loop (Basics, p. 12).

2 Open the loop of an earring wire (Basics). Attach the bead unit and close the loop. Make a second earring to match the first.

Structure
a beautiful
connection to
secure these
beads

Disk-bead bracelet

by Heather Boardman

With ingenious wire harnesses, you can connect disk beads to make a bracelet. What's more, the wire becomes an integral part of the bracelet's architecture. It's up to you which side of the bead shows (either side of the harness works as the front). Just make sure each bead unit faces the same way when you attach it.

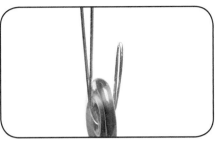

1 Cut a 4-in. (10 cm) piece of wire. Fold it in half. Over both ends, string a disk bead. Fold the wire around the bead, leaving about ¼ in. (6 mm) of the folded end extending beyond the bead.

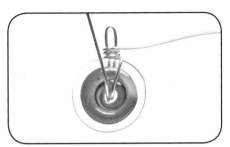

2 With one end, wrap the wire around the folded end as shown, making a loop. Trim the excess wrapping wire.

3 Wrap the other end around in the opposite direction, covering the previous wraps. Trim the excess wire.

Supplies

- **5-6** 15-20 mm disk beads (hmbstudios.com)
- 40-48 in. (1.0-1.2 m) 22-gauge half-hard wire
- **6-7** 5-6 mm jump rings
- **2-4** 3-4 mm jump rings
- toggle clasp
- chainnose and roundnose pliers, or **2** pairs of chainnose pliers
- diagonal wire cutters

4 Repeat steps 1 to 3 to make a second harness for the bead. Make two harnesses for each bead.

5 Open a 5-6 mm jump ring (Basics, p. 12). Attach two bead units. Close the jump ring.

Tips

- To save time, cut each wire and fold it in half before assembling the bracelet.
- Attach additional jump rings to lengthen the bracelet slightly.

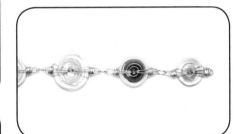

6 Use jump rings to attach all the bead units.

7 On each end, attach a 5-6 mm jump ring, one or two 3-4 mm jump rings, and half of a toggle clasp.

Phone charm won't

String some style for your cell

by Paula Radke

Whether you think they're indispensable or the scourge of mankind (or both), cell phones are everywhere. So let's make them pretty! These super-simple phone charms are made from my own dichroic beads. Not only do they add sparkle to your day, they make your phone easier to spot in your purse.

1 On a head pin, string a 3 mm round spacer and a 5 mm round spacer. Make a plain loop (Basics, p. 12). Make three spacer units.

2 Cut a 4-in. (10 cm) piece of wire. Make the first half of a wrapped loop (Basics). Attach the spacer units and complete the wraps.

3 On the wire, string: 5 mm dichroic bead, flat spacer, 7 mm dichroic bead, flat spacer, 13 mm dichroic bead, flat spacer, 7 mm bead, flat spacer, 5 mm bead. Make a wrapped loop.

waste your minutes

Supplies

Dichroic beads from Paula Radke
Dichroic Glass, paularadke.com.

- ◆ 13 mm round dichroic bead
- ◆ **2** 7 mm round dichroic beads
- ◆ **2** 5 mm round dichroic beads
- ◆ **4** 5 mm flat spacers
- ◆ **3** 5 mm round spacers
- ◆ **3** 3 mm round spacers
- ◆ 4 in. (10 cm) 20-gauge half-hard wire
- ◆ **3** 1½-in. (3.8 cm) head pins
- ◆ cell phone connector (Rings & Things, rings-things.com)
- ◆ name tag with jump ring (optional)
- ◆ chainnose and roundnose pliers
- ◆ diagonal wire cutters
- ◆ split-ring pliers (optional)

4 Attach the dangle to the split ring of a cell phone connector.

Tip

To personalize the charm, attach a stamped name tag or a dichroic charm with rub-on letters. Tags and personalized stamps are available from Microstamp, microstampusa.com.

Bead your way
to organization

Pretty smart idea

by Steven James

Disorganization isn't pretty, but keeping track of a pen at your desk or home office can be downright stylish. Gather just a few materials, including that little bowl of seed beads you don't have time to sort, and you'll have everything you need for a colorful pen leash. Best of all, you'll string it in less time than you spent looking for the last pen you lost.

1 With a push pin, poke a hole in the center of a pen cap. Remove the push pin.

2 Cut a 6-in. (15 cm) piece of 24-gauge wire. Make a wrapped loop (Basics, p. 12) on one end of the wire and string the pen cap on the wire.

3 Pull the wrapped loop against the inside of the cap. On the available end of the wire, string a spacer and make a wrapped loop.

4 Cut a piece of beading wire (Basics). String seed beads, interspersing 8–16 mm beads, until the strand is within 1 in. (2.5 cm) of the finished length.

On one end, string a crimp bead and the wrapped loop of the pen cap. Go back through the beads just strung and tighten the wire. Crimp the crimp bead (Basics) and trim the excess wire.

5 On the remaining end, string a crimp bead and 1 in. (2.5 cm) of seed beads. String the loop of the magnetic clip and go back through the crimp bead and a few adjacent beads. Tighten the wire and crimp the crimp bead. Trim the excess wire.

6 Use chainnose pliers to close a crimp cover over each crimp bead.

Supplies

- **8–10** assorted 8–16 mm beads
- 2 g assorted seed beads
- 5 mm spacer
- flexible beading wire, .014 or .015
- 6 in. (15 cm) 24-gauge half-hard wire
- **2** crimp beads
- **2** crimp covers
- pen with cap
- magnetic bulldog clip
- chainnose and roundnose pliers
- diagonal wire cutters
- push pin
- crimping pliers (optional)

Showcase a favorite bead in your décor

Fan and lamp pulls

by Joanna Mueller

Keep your lampworked beads on display by using them to create jazzy fan and lamp pulls. With such a wide variety of art beads available, you're sure to find one that matches your home décor.

Tip

If you want added security, apply adhesive (such as G-S Hypo Cement) to the threads of the bead end prior to attaching it in step 1.

Design alternative

For extra character, try replacing the split ring with a handmade wire coil.

1 Unscrew the bottom end of a bead holder. String: 4–5 mm spacer, 6 mm spacer, flat spacer, art bead, flat spacer. Reattach the bead end.

2 Use a split ring (Basics, p. 12) to attach the bead holder and a ball chain connector.
Cut a 3–6 in. (7.6–15 cm) piece of chain. Attach one end to the ball chain connector. Use chainnose pliers to close the connector firmly around the ball chain.

3 Attach the remaining end of the ball chain to a ball chain clasp. If necessary, use chainnose pliers to tighten the clasp around the ball chain.

Supplies

- 15–30 mm art bead (Joanna Mueller, sleekbeads.com)
- **2** 7–9 mm flat spacers
- 6 mm round spacer
- 4–5 mm round spacer
- 3–6 in. (7.6–15 cm) ball chain
- 1½–2 in. (3.8–5 cm) bead holder (Fire Mountain Gems and Beads, firemountaingems.com)
- 6 mm split ring
- ball chain connector (Rings & Things, rings-things.com)
- ball chain clasp (Rings & Things)
- chainnose pliers
- diagonal wire cutters

Metal

and chain

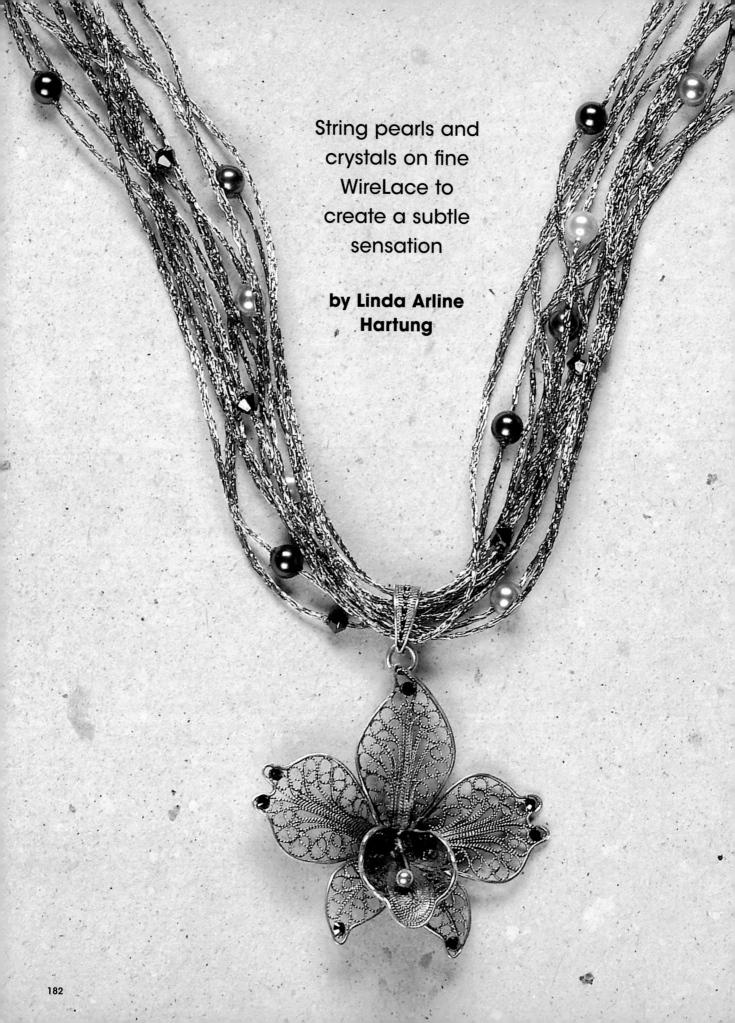

String pearls and crystals on fine WireLace to create a subtle sensation

by Linda Arline Hartung

Amazing greys

While shades of grey usually suggest uncertainty, the style of this sophisticated necklace-and-earring set is a sure thing. A white-to-black range of pearls and crystals float on smoky strands to create a perfect accent for a little black dress or a confident contrast to jeans.

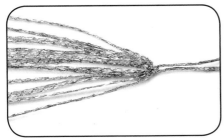

1 necklace • Decide how long you want your necklace to be. Double that measurement and cut six strands of WireLace to that length. Cut a 6-in. (15 cm) piece of WireLace. Use it to tie an overhand knot (Basics, p. 12) at the center of the six strands. Fold them in half and apply glue to the knot.

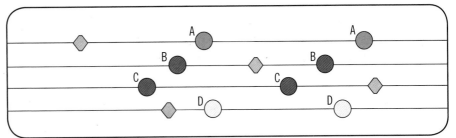

2 Twist the end of each of the 12 strands to form a point (apply glue to the point if necessary). Leaving a ½-in. (1.3 cm) gap in the center of the strands for a pendant, string the pearls and crystals on the strands as shown, staggering the pearls and crystals. Repeat the pattern until you have three strands of each pearl color. Apply glue next to each bead and slide the bead over the glue.

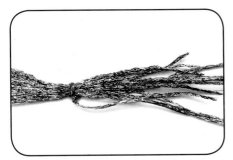

3 Gently pull the beaded strands together, making them even. Cut a 6-in. (15 cm) piece of WireLace and use it to tie an overhand knot 1 in. (2.5 cm) from the end of the strands. Apply glue to the knot.

4 On one side, trim the excess WireLace close to the knot. Prepare two-part epoxy and fill a bell end-cap half full. Insert the knot in the cap and let it dry. Repeat on the other end.

Tip

These are the colors I used in the project:

• WireLace: titanium

• Pearls: white, light grey, dark grey, black

• 3 mm bicone crystals: jet hematite AB2X

• 6 mm bicone crystals: jet hematite

> **"The best tip I can give readers is to visualize your design, experiment, and have fun."**

5 Center a pendant on the strands.

6 On each end, open the loop of the bell cap (Basics) and attach half of a clasp.

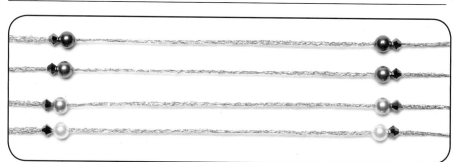

1 earrings • Cut four 4-in. (10 cm) pieces of WireLace. On each piece, string a bicone crystal, two pearls, and a bicone. Position the pearls 3 in. (7.6 cm) apart.

Mix two-part epoxy. Apply epoxy to the WireLace next to each bead and slide the bead over the epoxy. Trim the excess WireLace as close to the bicones as possible.

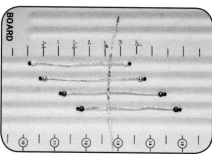

2 Cut a 4-in. (10 cm) piece of WireLace. Place it near the 2½-in. mark on a bead board or ruler. Line up the beaded strands at ½-in. (1.3 cm) intervals perpendicular to the 4-in. (10 cm) piece.

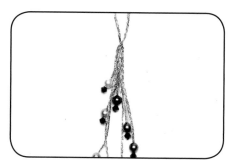

3 Using the 4-in. (10 cm) piece, tie the beaded strand together with an overhand knot (Basics, p. 12). Fold the strands at the knot and adjust them if necessary. Apply glue to the knot.

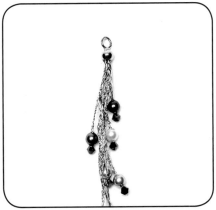

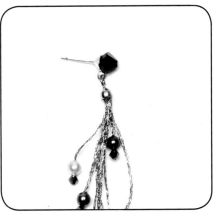

4 Trim the excess WireLace close to the knot. Prepare two-part epoxy and fill a bell end-cap half full. Insert the knot in the cap and let it dry.

5 Place an earring post in a piece of foam to hold it upright. Fill the earring cup half full with epoxy. Insert a top-drilled bicone hole-side down in the cup.

6 Open the loop of a bell cap (Basics) and attach the earring post. Make a second earring in the mirror image of the first.

Design alternative

For a softer look, choose different colors of WireLace and white pearls and crystals.

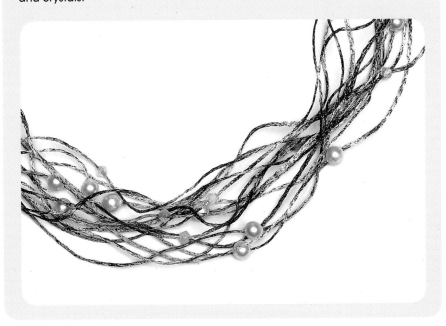

Supplies

necklace 17 in. (43 cm)
- 35 mm filigree pendant with large bail
- **24** 4 mm glass pearls in four colors
- **12** 3 mm bicone crystals
- 6 yd. (5.5 m) 1 mm WireLace
- **2** bell end-caps (Mimi's Gems, mimisgems.com)
- box clasp
- chainnose pliers
- two-part clear-drying epoxy

earrings
- **2** 6 mm bicone crystals, top drilled
- **16** 4 mm glass pearls in four colors
- **16** 3 mm bicone crystals
- 1 yd. (91 cm) 1 mm WireLace
- **2** bell end-caps (Mimi's Gems, mimisgems.com)
- 4 mm cup-and-loop earring posts with ear nuts (Mimi's Gems)
- chainnose pliers
- two-part clear-drying epoxy
- bead board or ruler
- scrap foam (optional)

A modern take on blue

Simple elements shine in a contemporary necklace, bracelet, and earrings

by Jennifer Ortiz

For a sleek geometric necklace, link bicone crystals and jump rings. You'll be making lots of wrapped loops, so practice with inexpensive copper wire (available from hardware stores) and refer to Basics, p. 12, if you need a quick refresher.

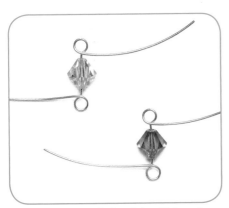

1 **necklace** • Cut a 3-in. (7.6 cm) piece of wire. Make the first half of a wrapped loop (Basics, p. 12) on one end. String a bicone crystal and make the first half of a wrapped loop. Make 25 to 29 bead units in two colors.

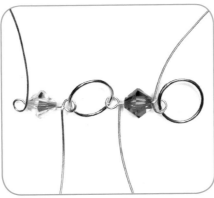

2 Attach one loop of a bead unit to a soldered jump ring. Attach one loop of another bead unit to the jump ring. Attach a soldered jump ring to one loop. Complete the wraps as you go, leaving the first loop unwrapped. Continue attaching bead units and soldered jump rings until the necklace is within 1 in. (2.5 cm) of the finished length, ending with an unwrapped loop.

3 Check the fit, and add or remove bead units or jump rings if necessary. Complete the wraps on the end loops.

On each end, open a 3–4 mm jump ring (Basics). Attach the end loop and half of a clasp. Close the jump ring.

4 On a head pin, string a spacer, a bicone, and a spacer. Make a wrapped loop.

5 Use a 3–4 mm jump ring to attach the bead unit to one of the end loops.

Design alternative

For an organic-looking necklace, use hammered jump rings. Simply place a soldered jump ring on a bench block or anvil, and hammer gently on both sides.

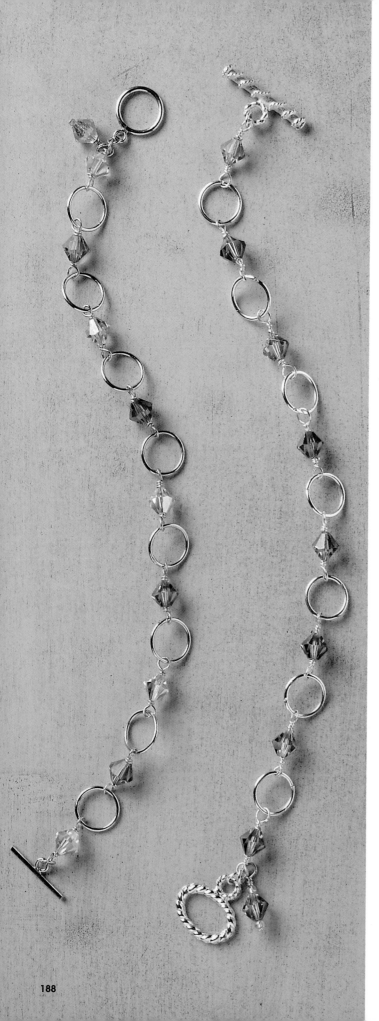

bracelet • Follow step 1 of the necklace, making eight or nine bead units. Follow steps 2–5.

1 **earrings** • On a head pin, string a spacer, a bicone crystal, and a spacer. Make the first half of a wrapped loop.

2 Cut a 3-in. (7.6 cm) piece of wire. Make the first half of a wrapped loop (Basics, p. 12) on one end. String a bicone and make the first half of a wrapped loop perpendicular to the first loop.

3 Attach the head pin unit to a soldered jump ring. Attach one loop of the remaining bead unit to the jump ring. Complete the wraps.

4 Open the loop of an earring wire (Basics). Attach the dangle and close the loop. Make a second earring to match the first.

patina

Patinated copper puts a necklace, bracelet, and earrings in blue mode

by Jane Konkel

Make an easy necklace by stringing a strand of beads through cool-blue chain. Suspending copper chain over ammonia turns it a rich shade of blue. Pass a short strand through the chain for a matching bracelet, and use patinated findings to make chandelier earrings.

Supplies

necklace 16 in. (41 cm)
- 8-in. (20 cm) strand 9 mm cathedral fire-polished crystals
- 16-in. (41 cm) strand 6–8 mm pearls
- **42–54** 3 mm faceted round spacers
- flexible beading wire, .014 or .015
- 16–20 in. (41–51 cm) copper chain, 20 mm links (Midwest Beads, midwestbeads.biz)
- **2** crimp beads
- S-hook clasp with **2** jump rings
- chainnose and roundnose pliers
- crimping pliers (optional)
- diagonal wire cutters

bracelet
- **3–4** 9 mm cathedral fire-polished crystals
- **12–15** 6–8 mm pearls
- **16–20** 3 mm faceted round spacers
- flexible beading wire, .014 or .015
- 6–8 in. (15–20 cm) copper chain, 20 mm links (Midwest Beads, midwestbeads.biz)
- **2–4** 5–6 mm jump rings (optional)
- **2** crimp beads
- S-hook clasp with **2** jump rings
- chainnose and roundnose pliers
- crimping pliers (optional)
- diagonal wire cutters

earrings
- **2** 9 mm cathedral fire-polished crystals
- **4** 6–8 mm pearls
- **6** 3 mm faceted round spacers
- pair of 40 mm copper chandelier findings (Fire Mountain Gems and Beads, firemountaingems.com)
- **6** 2-in. (5 cm) head pins
- pair of earring wires
- chainnose and roundnose pliers
- diagonal wire cutters

1 necklace • Cut a piece of beading wire (Basics, p. 12). On the wire, string: pearl, spacer, pearl, spacer, pearl, spacer, crystal. Repeat until the strand is within 2 in. (5 cm) of the finished length.

2 Cut a piece of chain to the length you want your necklace to be. Prepare the chain (see New technique, p. 192). Pass the strand down through one link and up through the next until you've strung the entire chain.

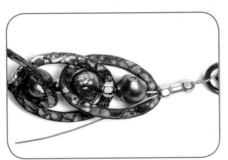

3 On each end of the beaded strand, string a spacer, a crimp bead, a spacer, and a jump ring. Check the fit, and add or remove beads if necessary. Go back through the beads just strung and tighten the wire. Crimp the crimp bead (Basics) and trim the excess wire.

4 On each end, open the jump ring (Basics) and attach the chain and the S-hook clasp. Close the jump ring.

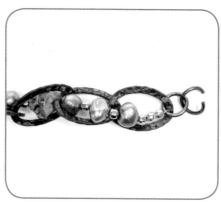

bracelet • Follow steps 1–4 of the necklace. To adjust the length of your bracelet, attach additional jump rings to one end.

1 earrings • On a head pin, string a crystal and a spacer. Make the first half of a wrapped loop (Basics, p. 12). Repeat to make two pearl units.

2 Prepare two chandelier findings (see New technique, below). Attach the crystal unit to the center loop of a chandelier finding. Attach each pearl unit to an outer loop. Complete the wraps.

3 Open the loop of an earring wire (Basics). Attach the dangle and close the loop. Make a second earring to match the first.

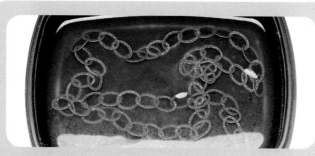

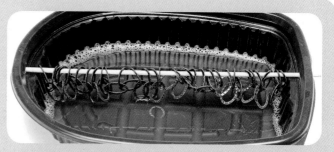

New technique

To add a blue patina to copper:

1) Soak copper pieces in a saltwater solution (approximately 2 Tbsp. salt per 4 oz. water) for four to eight hours.

2) Hang the copper pieces from a dowel that you've cut to fit the rim of a plastic container.

3) Fill the bottom of the container with about ½ in. (1.3 cm) of ammonia (keep the ammonia from touching the copper).

4) Cover with a tight-fitting lid and set aside for four to ten hours.

5) In a ventilated area, spray dry pieces with a protective matte finish, such as Krylon (available at craft or hardware stores).

Modern
metal earrings

Mix chain styles for an edgy look

by Gretta Van Someren

Chain, links, and jump rings give these easy earrings a modern edge. You can combine different metal finishes or keep it simple with a single type.

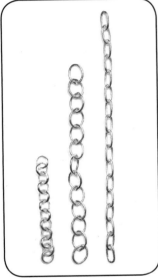

1 Cut a 1-in. (2.5 cm), a 2-in. (5 cm), and a 2¼-in. (5.7 cm) piece of chain, each in a different style.

2 Open a 4–5 mm jump ring (Basics, p. 12). Attach a charm or drop and the 1-in. (2.5 cm) piece of chain. Close the jump ring.

3 Use a 4–5 mm jump ring to attach all three chains. Use an 8–9 mm jump ring to attach the 4–5 mm jump ring and a link.

4 Use a 4–5 mm jump ring to attach the 8–9 mm jump ring and the loop of an earring wire. Make a second earring the mirror image of the first.

Supplies

- **2** 10–20 mm charms or drops
- **2** 10–12 mm links, washers, or soldered jump rings
- **1** ft. (30 cm) chain, 4–6 mm links, in three styles
- **2** 8–9 mm jump rings
- **6** 4–5 mm jump rings
- pair of lever-back earring wires
- chainnose and roundnose pliers, or **2** pairs of chainnose pliers
- diagonal wire cutters

Tips

- If you like your metals dark, use liver of sulfur to oxidize the chain and findings.
- You can either look for individual links, washers, or soldered jump rings or cut a few links of chain left over from previous projects.

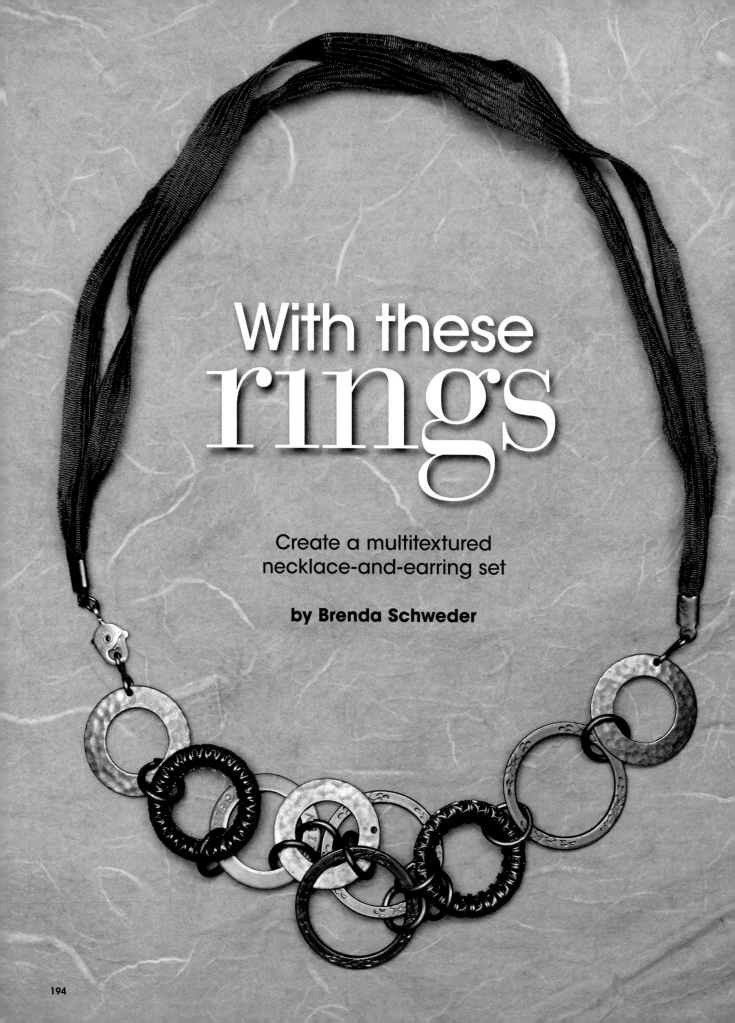

With these
rings

Create a multitextured
necklace-and-earring set

by Brenda Schweder

When I saw these different rings, I knew they were meant to be together. The textures play off each other beautifully, and the softness of the ribbon feels as good as it looks. I loved the front-hooking clasp so much, I used it again in matching earrings.

Supplies

All components from Vintaj Natural Brass Co., vintaj.com.

necklace 18 in. (46 cm)
- **3** 25 mm "garden" rings
- **2** 24 mm filigree rings
- **2** 23 mm "believe" rings
- **2** 22 mm hammered rings
- 24–26 in. (61–66 cm) 8 mm ribbon
- **10** 10–15 mm jump rings
- **4–6** mm jump ring
- **2** 9 mm figure 8 connectors
- **2** 9 mm crimp ends
- lobster claw clasp
- chainnose and roundnose pliers, or **2** pairs of chainnose pliers
- E6000 adhesive

earrings
- **2** 22 mm hammered rings
- **4** 4–6 mm jump rings
- **2** lobster claw clasps
- pair of lever-back earring wires
- chainnose and roundnose pliers, or **2** pairs of chainnose pliers

1 necklace • Open 10 10–15 mm jump rings (Basics, p. 12). Attach two hammered rings, two filigree rings, two "believe" rings, and three "garden" rings as shown. Close the jump rings as you go.

2 Open a loop of a figure 8 connector. Attach one end of the ring section and close the loop. Repeat on the other end.

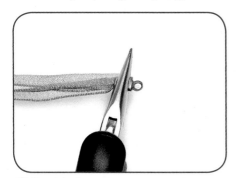

3 Decide how long you want your necklace to be. Subtract the length of the ring section and cut a piece of ribbon twice that length. Fold the ribbon in half lengthwise. Apply glue to one end and fold the ribbon widthwise, then attach a crimp end (Basics). Repeat on the other end.

4 Use a 4–6 mm jump ring to attach a crimp end and the clasp.

5 Open a loop of the figure 8 connector on the remaining end of the ring section. Attach the remaining crimp end and close the loop.

66Believe in your style and your stuff. If you follow your heart's desire, that's when things really start to happen for you.99

1 earrings • Open a jump ring (Basics, p. 12). Attach a hammered ring and a clasp. Close the jump ring.

2 Use a jump ring to attach an earring wire and the dangle. Make a second earring to match the first.

Tip

Choose your jump ring sizes based on how much movement you want the ring section to have. Larger jump rings will give the piece more flow; smaller jump rings offer more stability.

Design alternative

Use crystal-ring pendants for a dressed-up, night-on-the-town look.

Sometimes LESS Says MORE

A few well-chosen beads highlight an asymmetrical chain necklace and earrings

by Debbi Simon

A necklace strung with briolettes is a stylish statement, but you don't need an entire strand to make your point. A few briolettes dangled from three types of chain speak volumes. Cinch the chains together with extra-large jump rings for an asymmetrical design.

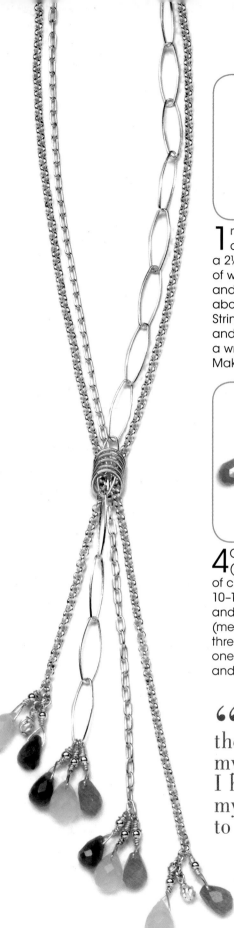

1 necklace • To make a briolette unit: Cut a 2½-in. (6.4 cm) piece of wire. String a briolette and make a set of wraps above it (Basics, p. 12). String a 3 mm spacer and make the first half of a wrapped loop (Basics). Make 10 briolette units.

2 To make a spacer unit: On a head pin, string a textured spacer. Make the first half of a wrapped loop. Make two units.

3 Cut two 10–14-in. (25–36 cm) pieces of 2–4 mm (small) link chain. On one end of each piece, attach a spacer unit and complete the wraps. Attach two briolette units and complete the wraps.

4 Cut two 10–14-in. (25–36 cm) pieces of chain, one with 10–16 mm (large) links and one with 4–8 mm (medium) links. Attach three briolette units to one end of each piece and complete the wraps.

5 Slide five or six 10 mm jump rings over the ends of all four chains.

6 Open a 5 mm jump ring (Basics) and attach a small-link chain, the medium-link chain, and a lobster claw clasp. Close the jump ring. Repeat on the other side with the remaining chains, substituting a 10 mm jump ring for the clasp.

❝When I try to apply formal theories and rules of color to my designs, it holds me back. I have learned to just go with my gut, and happily, it seems to work.**❞**

1 earrings • Cut a ¾-in. (1.9 cm) piece of 2–4 mm (small) link chain, a ½-in. (1.3 cm) piece of 4–8 mm (medium) link chain, and a ½-in. (1.3 cm) piece of 10–16 mm (large) link chain. Open a 10 mm jump ring (Basics, p. 12) and attach each chain. Close the jump ring.

2 Make three briolette units and a spacer unit as in steps 1 and 2 of the necklace. Attach two briolette units to the medium chain. Attach a briolette unit and the spacer unit to the large chain. Complete the wraps as you go.

3 Open the loop of an earring wire (Basics) and attach the dangle. Close the loop. Make a second earring in the mirror image of the first.

Supplies

necklace 24 in. (61 cm)
- **10** 10–15 mm briolettes in two or three colors
- **2** 5 mm textured spacers
- **10** 3 mm spacers
- 25 in. (64 cm) 24-gauge half-hard wire
- 10–14 in. (25–36 cm) chain, 10–16 mm links
- 10–14 in. (25–36 cm) chain, 4–8 mm links
- 20–28 in. (51–71 cm) chain, 2–4 mm links
- **2** 1½-in. (3.8 cm) head pins
- **6** or **7** 10 mm jump rings
- **2** 5 mm jump rings
- lobster claw clasp
- chainnose and roundnose pliers
- diagonal wire cutters

earrings
- **6** 10–15 mm briolettes, in two or three colors
- **2** 5 mm textured spacers
- **6** 3 mm spacers
- 15 in. (38 cm) 24-gauge half-hard wire
- 1 in. (2.5 cm) chain, 10–16 mm links
- 1 in. (2.5 cm) chain, 4–8 mm links
- 1½ in. (3.8 cm) chain, 2–4 mm links
- **2** 1½-in. (3.8 cm) head pins
- **2** 10 mm jump rings
- pair of earring wires
- chainnose and roundnose pliers
- diagonal wire cutters

Design alternative

For quick earrings, use a long link of chain, a briolette, and 6–8 in. (15–20 cm) of wire.

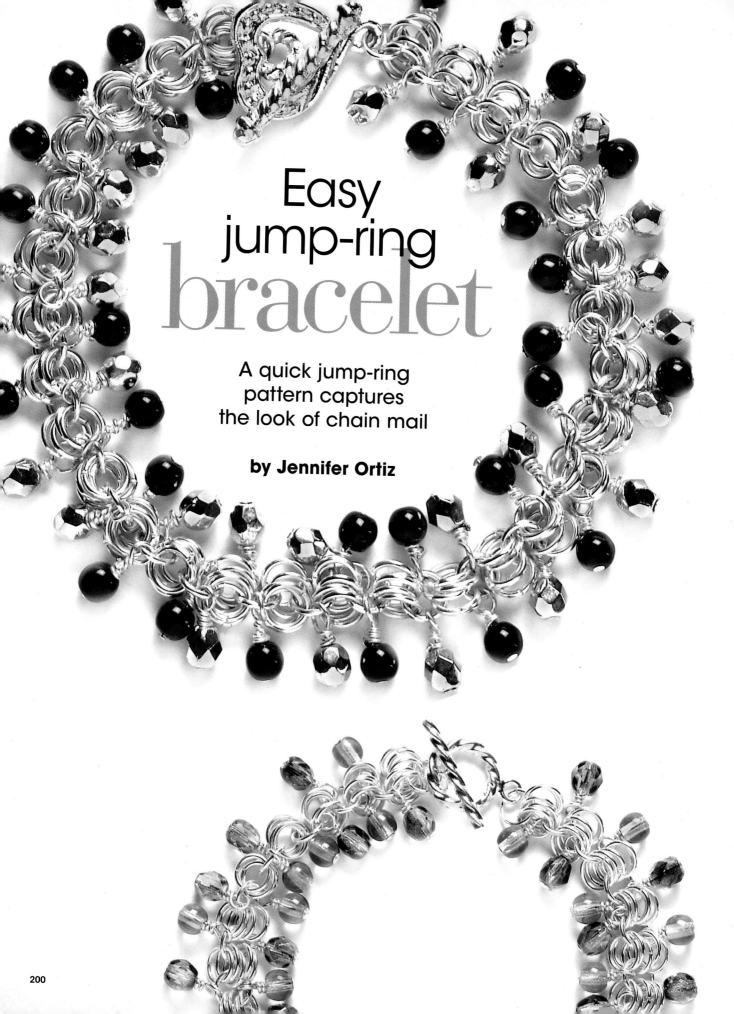

Easy
jump-ring
bracelet

A quick jump-ring pattern captures the look of chain mail

by Jennifer Ortiz

Do you love the look of chain mail but feel intimidated by the complicated weaves? Ease your way into jump-ring jewelry with this stylish bracelet-and-earring set. The pattern is simple, and tiny glass beads add a touch of color.

1 bracelet • Open a jump ring (Basics, p. 12). Pick up 10 closed jump rings and close the jump ring.

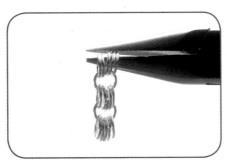

2 Use a second jump ring to attach five jump rings from the first jump-ring unit and five additional jump rings.

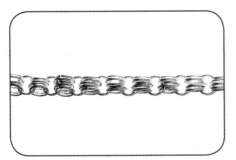

3 Continue attaching connecting rings (the single rings between the groups of five) and jump rings in groups of five until the bracelet is within 1 in. (2.5 cm) of the finished length. End with a group of five jump rings.

4 On a head pin, string a 4 mm bead. Make the first half of a wrapped loop (Basics). Repeat with a 4 mm bead in a second color.

Count how many connecting rings are in your bracelet. Make a bead unit in each color for each connecting ring.

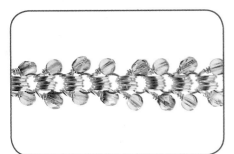

5 Attach two bead units, one in each color, to each connecting ring on either side. Alternate the colors and complete the wraps as you go.

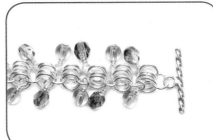

6 Use a jump ring to attach one end of the bracelet and half of a clasp. Repeat on the other end.

Supplies

bracelet
- **50-62** 4 mm beads in two colors
- **50-62** 1½-in. (3.8 cm) 24-gauge head pins
- **157-193** 5 mm 22-gauge jump rings
- toggle clasp
- **2** pairs of chainnose pliers or chainnose and bentnose pliers
- roundnose pliers
- diagonal wire cutters

earrings
- **2** 4 mm beads
- **2** 1½-in. (3.8 cm) 24-gauge head pins
- **22** 4 mm 20.5-gauge jump rings
- pair of earring wires
- **2** pairs of chainnose pliers or chainnose and bentnose pliers
- roundnose pliers
- diagonal wire cutters

Tip

When you buy jump rings, they will not be tightly closed. Close all but about 30 of your jump rings before you begin the project. That way you won't have to stop and adjust the jump rings as you work.

1 earrings • Open two jump rings (Basics, p. 12). Attach two more jump rings and close the jump rings. Make a second jump-ring unit.

2 Open three jump rings and connect the two jump-ring units. Close the jump rings.

3 On a head pin, string a 4 mm bead. Make a wrapped loop (Basics).

4 Open a jump ring on one end of the jump-ring unit. Attach the bead unit and close the jump ring.

5 Open the loop of an earring wire (Basics). Attach the dangle and close the loop. Make a second earring to match the first.

Design alternative

For added drama, incorporate colored jump rings into your design. Colored jump rings are available from Fire Mountain Gems and Beads (firemountaingems.com) and The Ring Lord (theringlord.com).

Coiled collar

Create and link custom shapes for an artistic statement

by Louise Jeremich

Looking for a challenging project? This necklace may be just the ticket. To create this elaborate collar, form three coil designs using heavy-gauge wire. Position the hammered coils in a mirrored pattern and join them with thinner wire.

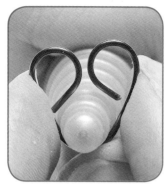

1 To make a heart coil: Cut two 3-in. (7.6 cm) pieces of 16-gauge wire. Pair the wires. Wrap one end of the pair around the round tip of a mandrel to make a loop. Repeat on the other end.

Center the pair on the mandrel's second tier, and pull the loops together to form a heart shape. Use roundnose pliers to tighten each loop's center. Make two heart coils.

2 To make a type A coil: Cut two 5¼-in. (13.3 cm) pieces of 16-gauge wire. Pair the wires. Wrap one end of the pair around the mandrel's tip. Make two successively larger wraps, by using larger tiers of the mandrel. Flatten the coils.

Repeat on the remaining end, wrapping the wire in the opposite direction. Use roundnose pliers to tighten each coil's center. Make four type A coils.

3 To make a type B coil: Cut two 6-in. (15 cm) pieces of 16-gauge wire. Pair the wires. Wrap the ends of the pair as in step 2. If desired, make the bottom coil larger than the top coil. Make two type B coils.

4 To make a clasp: Cut a 4-in. (10 cm) piece of 16-gauge wire. On each end, use roundnose pliers to make a small loop. Place one end on the mandrel and pull the wire around. Repeat on the remaining end in the opposite direction.

5 Cut a 2-in. (5 cm) piece of 16-gauge wire. On each end, make a small loop. Center the wire on the mandrel. Pull the loop ends toward each other until they overlap.

On a bench block or anvil, hammer one half of the clasp. Turn the piece over and hammer the other side. Repeat with the remaining half of the clasp and each coil.

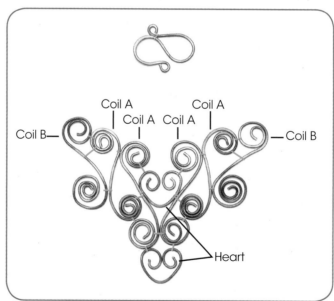

Coil A Coil A Coil A Coil A
Coil B — — Coil B
Heart

6 To attach the coils: Cut 19 3-in. (7.6 cm) pieces of 26-gauge wire. Wrap one piece tightly around the hook clasp as shown. Trim the excess wire. Use chainnose pliers to tuck in the ends.

Attach the remaining coils as shown. Hammer the entire centerpiece.

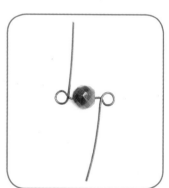

7 To make a chain-and-bead section: Cut a 2½-in. (6.4 cm) piece of 24-gauge wire. Make the first half of a wrapped loop (Basics, p. 12) on one end. String a bead and make the first half of a wrapped loop. Make ten to 12 bead units.

8 Cut two 1-in. (2.5 cm) and six to eight 2-in. (5 cm) pieces of chain. On each side, attach a bead unit's loop to the top coil of the B-coil. Attach the remaining loop to a 1-in. (2.5 cm) chain. Complete the wraps as you go.

Attach a bead unit's loop to the large bottom coil of the B-coil. Attach the remaining loop to a 2-in. (5 cm) chain.

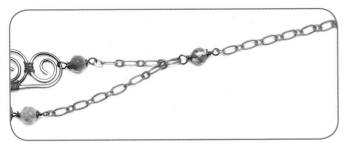

9 On each side, attach one loop of a bead unit to both chains. Attach the remaining loop to a 2-in. (5 cm) chain.

Attach a bead unit, chain, and a bead unit. Leave the end loop unwrapped.

10 Check the fit. If necessary, trim chain or attach a chain or bead unit on each end. On each end, attach half of the clasp.

Supplies

necklace 21 in. (53 cm)
- **10–12** 6–8 mm beads
- 4 ft. (1.2 m) 16-gauge copper or Artistic wire
- 25–30 in. (64–76 cm) 24-gauge copper or Artistic wire
- 5 ft. (1.5 m) 26-gauge copper or Artistic wire
- 14–18 in. (36–46 cm) chain, 3–4 mm links
- chainnose and roundnose pliers
- diagonal wire cutters
- bench block or anvil
- Fiskars Right Angle mandrel (fiskarscrafts.com)
- hammer

Tip

Whether you form coils with a mandrel or roundnose pliers, work with two wires at once. This will help you make symmetrical coils.

Tiers of Joy

Teardrop components frame simple earrings

by Karey Grant

I want to wear earrings that are light in weight but heavy in impact. Delicate teardrop lines are always elegant and offer an opportunity to frame a gemstone. My favorite stones are neutrals — citrine, smoky quartz, and aquamarine — but any gemstone will add expression to your design.

1 Cut a 7-in. (18 cm) piece of wire. String a briolette and cross the ends above it, leaving a 3/8-in. (1 cm) stem. With the stem, make a plain loop (Basics, p. 12) perpendicular to the briolette.

2 Grasping the plain loop with chainnose pliers, use your fingers to wrap the wire around the top of the briolette. Trim the excess wire. Use chainnose pliers to tuck the end under the wraps. Open the plain loop (Basics) and attach the inner loop of a teardrop component. Close the loop.

3 Cut a 3-in. (7.6 cm) piece of wire. Make the first half of a wrapped loop on one end. String a spacer and make the first half of a wrapped loop (Basics).

4 Attach one loop of the spacer unit and the outer loop of the teardrop-and-briolette component. Attach the remaining loop of the spacer unit and the inner loop of another teardrop component. Complete the wraps.

5 Open the loop of an earring wire (Basics) and attach the dangle. Close the loop. Make a second earring to match the first.

Supplies

- ◆ 4 42 mm teardrop components (The Bead Shop, beadshop.com)
- ◆ 2 10–14 mm briolettes
- ◆ 2 3–4 mm spacers
- ◆ 20 in. (51 cm) 24-gauge half-hard wire
- ◆ pair of earring wires
- ◆ chainnose and roundnose pliers
- ◆ diagonal wire cutters

Tips

- • If you use smaller briolettes, wrap them with 26-gauge wire. In step 1, make the first half of a wrapped loop instead of a plain loop. Attach the teardrop component in step 2 and wrap both wires when you complete the wraps.
- • For added texture, gently hammer the wire components.

Design alternative

Try other shapes of wire components and beads. I used marquise-shaped cubic zirconias from BeadFX, beadfx.com.

66 What I always remind my students is that you can worry or you can bead, but you should never, ever combine the two. **99**

Pearls

Bring a collection of
extra pearls together
for a unified design

Lovely

by Kerry Melson

Even if you've only been beading for a short time, you've undoubtedly amassed a small mountain of extra beads. Here's an opportunity to reduce the stockpile. Before you go out and purchase full strands of pearls, explore your mountain — pick out different colors, shapes, and sizes. You'll be pleased at how smartly leftover pearls come together to form an astonishing necklace and earrings.

1 necklace • Cut a 2½-in. (6.4 cm) piece of wire. Make a wrapped loop (Basics, p. 12) on one end. String a 7–12 mm (large) pearl and make a wrapped loop. Make eight to 10 large-pearl units.

2 Cut a 2½-in. (6.4 cm) piece of wire. Make a wrapped loop on one end. String a bead cap, a large pearl, and a bead cap. Make a wrapped loop. Make eight to 10 bead-cap units.

3 On a head pin, string spacers, bead caps, and one to three 2–6 mm pearls as desired. Make a wrapped loop. Make 45 to 60 small-pearl units.

4 Open a jump ring (Basics). Attach a bead-cap unit, three small-pearl units, and a large-pearl unit. Close the jump ring.

leftovers

5 Attach the remaining units and jump rings on each side of the first bead-cap unit, until the strand is within 1 in. (2.5 cm) of the finished length. End with a bead-cap unit.

6 Check the fit, and add or remove bead units or jump rings if necessary. Use a jump ring to attach half of a clasp to each end.

Supplies

necklace (gold necklace 19 in./48 cm; silver necklace 16 in./41 cm)

- ◆ **16–20** 7–12 mm (large) pearls in assorted colors and shapes
- ◆ **50–75** 2–6 mm (small) pearls in assorted colors and shapes
- ◆ **16–20** 4–5 mm flat or saucer-shaped spacers
- ◆ **16–20** 3–4 mm round spacers
- ◆ **20–40** 4–10 mm bead caps in assorted shapes
- ◆ 40–50 in. (1–1.3 m) 24-gauge half-hard wire
- ◆ **48–60** 1½-in. (3.8 cm) head pins
- ◆ **18–22** 6–8 mm oval jump rings
- ◆ toggle clasp
- ◆ chainnose and roundnose pliers
- ◆ diagonal wire cutters

earrings

- ◆ **2** 7–12 mm (large) pearls
- ◆ **8** 2–6 mm (small) pearls in four colors
- ◆ **2** 3–4 mm round spacers
- ◆ **2** 4–10 mm bead caps
- ◆ **10** 1½-in. (3.8 cm) head pins
- ◆ **4** 6–8 mm oval jump rings
- ◆ pair of earring wires
- ◆ chainnose and roundnose pliers
- ◆ diagonal wire cutters

Tip

To save time, cut all of the 2½-in. (6.4 cm) pieces of wire for the large-pearl units and the bead-cap units. Make a wrapped loop on one end of each piece, then string the beads.

1 earrings • On a head pin, string a 7–12 mm (large) pearl, a bead cap, and a round spacer. Make a wrapped loop (Basics, p. 12).

On a head pin, string a 2–6 mm (small) pearl and make a wrapped loop. Make four small-pearl units.

2 Open a jump ring (Basics). Attach the large-pearl unit and two small-pearl units. Close the jump ring.

3 Use another jump ring to attach the first jump ring and two small-pearl units.

4 Open the loop of an earring wire (Basics). Attach the dangle and close the loop. Make a second earring to match the first.

Design alternative

Make a scaled-down version of the necklace. Make seven bead-cap units and 14 small-pearl units. Use jump rings to connect the units and attach chain to each end of the strand.

"I bought my first beads from a jewelry designer who was clearing out her overstock. I was mesmerized by them. Thus began my love of beads."

Subtle&classic

A variety of colors brightens up a chain-and-pearl jewelry set

by Jackie Boettcher

Combine pearls and dainty bar-and-link chain for an elegant necklace, bracelet, and earrings. But remember — elegance should have a personality. Raise the stakes on this classic look by using pearls in many hues. (One of my sets uses eight different colors.) The result will be a subtle spectrum that makes otherwise grown-up jewelry a little sassy.

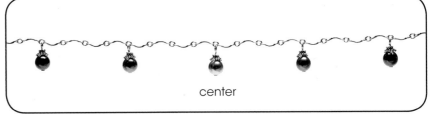

center

1 necklace • On a head pin, string a pearl and a bead cap. Make a plain loop (Basics, p. 12). Make twelve pearl units.

2 Cut an 8½-in. (21.6 cm) piece of chain. (The chain should have an even number of bars.) Open the loop of a pearl unit (Basics) and attach it to the center link. Close the loop. Repeat twice on each side, attaching a pearl unit every 1–1½ in. (2.5–3.8 cm).

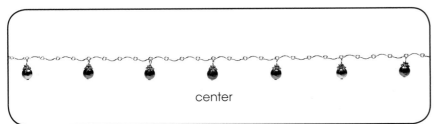

center

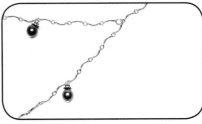

3 Decide how long you want your necklace to be and cut a piece of chain to that length. (The chain should have an even number of bars.) Attach a pearl unit to the center link. Repeat three times on each side, attaching a pearl unit every 1–1½ in. (2.5–3.8 cm).

4 On each side, open a 4–5 mm jump ring (Basics). Attach one end of the short chain to a link on the long chain about 2 in. (5 cm) beyond the last pearl unit. Close the jump ring.

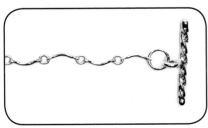

5 Check the fit and trim chain from each end if necessary. On each end, use a 5–6 mm jump ring to attach half of a clasp.

Tip

If you choose a multihued color scheme, consider buying your pearls individually, so it's easy to choose a variety of colors while buying only what you need.

Supplies

necklace 16 in. (41 cm)
- **12** 6 mm pearls
- **12** 5–6 mm bead caps
- **24–28 in. (61–71 cm)** bar-and-link chain, 7–10 mm bars
- **12** 1-in. (2.5 cm) head pins
- **2** 5–6 mm jump rings
- **2** 4–5 mm jump rings
- toggle clasp
- chainnose and roundnose pliers
- diagonal wire cutters

bracelet
- **5** 6 mm pearls
- **5** 5–6 mm bead caps
- **18–24 in. (46–61 cm)** bar-and-link chain, 7–10 mm bars
- **5** 1-in. (2.5 cm) head pins
- **2** 4–6 mm jump rings
- lobster claw clasp and soldered jump ring
- chainnose and roundnose pliers
- diagonal wire cutters

earrings
- **6** 6 mm pearls
- **3 in. (7.6 cm)** bar-and-link chain, 7–10 mm bars
- **6** 1-in. (2.5 cm) head pins
- **6** 3–4 mm jump rings
- **2** three-to-one connectors or three-loop chandelier findings
- pair of earring wires
- chainnose and roundnose pliers
- diagonal wire cutters

1 bracelet • On a head pin, string a pearl and a bead cap. Using the largest part of your roundnose pliers, make a plain loop (Basics, p. 12). Make five pearl units.

2 Decide how long you want your bracelet to be and cut three pieces of chain to that length. (Each chain should have an even number of bars.) Open the loop of a pearl unit (Basics) and attach it to the center link of all three chains. Close the loop.

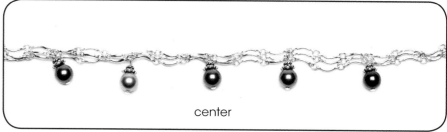

center

3 On each side, attach a pearl unit to all three chains 1 in. (2.5 cm) from the center. Repeat.

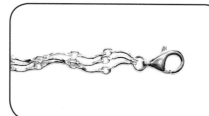

4 On one end, open a jump ring (Basics) and attach a lobster claw clasp and the three links of chain. Close the jump ring. On the other end, attach a jump ring to the three end lengths.

Design alternative

For an extra challenge, try substituting simple chain mail for bar-and-link chain. Using 5 mm jump rings, make stacks of three jump rings and connect the stacks with a single jump ring. Attach the pearls to the single rings.

1 earrings • On a head pin, string a pearl and make a plain loop (Basics, p. 12). Make three pearl units.

2 Cut three bars of chain. Open the loop of a pearl unit (Basics) and attach it to one end of a bar. Close the loop. Repeat with the remaining pearl units.

3 Open a jump ring (Basics) and attach a bar to the loop of a connector or chandelier finding. Close the jump ring. Repeat with the remaining bars.

4 Open the loop of an earring wire (Basics) and attach the dangle. Close the loop. Make a second earring to match the first.

A pearl's

Inlaid crystals make a pearl pendant and earrings sparkle ◆ **by Irina Miech**

Okay, they're not diamonds, but the twinkle of crystals set in these oval pearls are the perfect companion to its natural gleam. Smaller button pearls joined by bits of chain are a great support system for this elegant pairing.

1 necklace • On a head pin, string a 15 mm (large) pearl. Make a wrapped loop (Basics, p. 12).

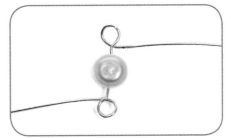

2 Cut a 2-in. (5 cm) piece of wire. Make the first half of a wrapped loop. String a 5 mm (small) pearl and make the first half of a wrapped loop. Make 20 to 26 small-pearl units.

3 Attach one loop of a small-pearl unit to the large-pearl unit. Complete the wraps.

4 Attach two small-pearl units to the dangle from step 3. Complete the wraps nearest the dangle.

5 Cut a ¼-in. (6 mm) piece of chain and attach one of the open loops. Complete the wraps.
Attach a small-pearl unit to the end link. Complete the wraps nearest the chain. Repeat on the other side.

6 Repeat step 5 until the necklace is the finished length. End with an unwrapped loop. Check the fit, and add or remove pearl units and chains from each end if necessary.
On one end, attach a lobster claw clasp to the remaining loop. Complete the wraps.

best friend

7 To make an extender: On a head pin, string a small pearl. Make a wrapped loop.

8 Attach the head-pin unit to a loop of a small-pearl unit. Attach three more small-pearl units, starting with the remaining loop and completing the wraps as you go. End with an unwrapped loop.

Attach the extender to the remaining end of the necklace. Complete the wraps. The lobster claw clasp uses a pearl as a stopper instead of connecting to a loop or chain link.

Design alternative

If time's at a premium, skip the loops and the chain and string tiny glass pearls and 4 mm bicone crystals in coordinating colors.

Tips

• Though I usually cut 3-in. (7.6 cm) pieces of wire for bead units, 2-in. (5 cm) pieces will be long enough, and you'll waste less wire.

• Take extra care when checking the fit of the necklace. The extender chain is strictly decorative and can't be used to adjust the length.

Supplies

All supplies from Eclectica, eclecticabeads.com (click on bead kits).

necklace 17 in. (43 cm)
◆ 15 mm crystal-inlaid pearl
◆ 16-in. (41 cm) strand 5 mm button pearls
◆ 4½ ft. (1.4 m) 24-gauge half-hard wire
◆ 6–8 in. (15–20 cm) cable chain, 2–3 mm links
◆ **2** 1½-in. (3.8 cm) head pins
◆ lobster claw clasp
◆ chainnose and roundnose pliers
◆ diagonal wire cutters

earrings
◆ **2** 15 mm crystal-inlaid pearls
◆ **2** 5 mm button pearls
◆ 4 in. (10 cm) 24-gauge half-hard wire
◆ **2** 1½-in. (3.8 cm) head pins
◆ pair of earring wires
◆ chainnose and roundnose pliers
◆ diagonal wire cutters

earrings • Make a large-pearl unit and a small-pearl unit following necklace steps 1 and 2. Follow step 3 to attach the units.

Open the loop of an earring wire (Basics, p. 12). Attach the dangle and close the loop. Make a second earring to match the first.

Multiple gemstone and pearl
strands create a lush look

by **Juliana Thaens**

Substantial style
with a twist

Combine seven strands of gemstones and pearls for an eye-catching necklace that is bound to be noticed. Twist the necklace before you put it on, and it will gleam with luster and color. Keep the earrings simple so that they don't compete with the necklace; lentil drops do the trick.

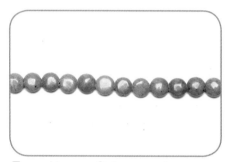

1 necklace • Cut seven pieces of beading wire (Basics, p. 12). On one wire, string lentil beads until the strand is within 1 in. (2.5 cm) of the finished length.

2 On the remaining wires, string beads until the strands are within 1 in. (2.5 cm) of the finished length. Set aside two pearls for step 7.

3 On each end of three wires, string a spacer. Over all three wires, string a crimp tube and a soldered jump ring or split ring.

4 On each end of two wires, string a spacer. Over both wires, string a crimp tube and a soldered jump ring. Repeat with the two remaining wires.

Supplies

necklace 16 in. (41 cm)
- 16-in. (41 cm) strand 8-10 mm gemstone lentil beads
- 16-in. (41 cm) strand 4-6 mm gemstone beads
- **5** 16-in. (41 cm) strands 3-7 mm pearls, assorted shapes
- **15** 3-4 mm round spacers
- flexible beading wire, .014 or .015
- 2-in. (5 cm) head pin
- **2** 8-10 mm jump rings
- **6** 5-6 mm soldered jump rings or split rings
- **6** 2 mm crimp tubes
- 18-20 mm lobster claw clasp
- 2 in. (5 cm) chain for extender, 5-7 mm links
- chainnose and roundnose pliers
- crimping pliers
- diagonal wire cutters

earrings
- **2** 8-10 mm gemstone lentil beads
- **2** 1½-in. (3.8 cm) decorative head pins
- **2** 5-6 mm soldered jump rings
- pair of earring wires
- chainnose and roundnose pliers
- diagonal wire cutters

5 Check the fit of all seven strands, and add or remove beads if necessary. Go back through the beads just strung and tighten the wires. Make folded crimps (Basics) and trim the excess wire.

6 Open a large jump ring (Basics) and attach the three soldered jump rings and a lobster claw clasp on one side. Close the jump ring. Repeat on the other side, substituting a 2-in. (5 cm) piece of chain for the clasp.

7 On a head pin, string a spacer and two pearls. Make the first half of a wrapped loop (Basics). Attach the bead unit to the chain and complete the wraps.

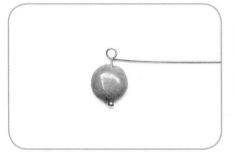

1 earrings • On a decorative head pin, string a lentil bead and make the first half of a wrapped loop (Basics, p. 12).

2 Attach the bead unit to a soldered jump ring and complete the wraps.

3 Open the loop of an earring wire (Basics). Attach the dangle and close the loop. Make a second earring to match the first.

Design alternative

To add sparkle, incorporate faceted glass and crystal into the strands.

Tip

If you want your necklace to be significantly longer than 16 in. (41 cm), double the number of gemstone and pearl strands you buy. If you only want to add a little length, string two to four extra beads on each end of the strands. As long as the extra beads match the general color scheme, they don't need to be an exact match.

"I am inspired by the beads themselves. I buy lots of things I think are beautiful and then get them home and see what looks great next to what."

Beach-style beauties

Preserve a day at the beach with a seaside set

by Irina Miech

On your next trip to the beach, leave the seashells in the sand with your footprints. Instead, pick up a few metal beach-themed charms. Combine them with symmetrical glass pearls, and you'll have one fin up on any mermaid.

1 necklace • Open a jump ring (Basics, p. 12) and attach a charm. Close the jump ring. Repeat with the remaining charms.

2 Cut a piece of beading wire (Basics). Center a charm unit on the wire.

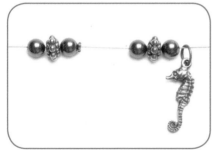

3 On each end, string a 6 mm pearl, an 8 mm spacer, a 6 mm pearl, and a 3 mm spacer. Repeat, substituting a charm unit for the 3 mm spacer.

4 On each end, string a 6 mm pearl and a metal accent bead. String 3 mm pearls until the strand is within 1 in. (2.5 cm) of the finished length.

5 On each end, string a crimp bead and half of a clasp. Check the fit, and add or remove beads from each end if necessary. Go back through the last few beads strung and tighten the wire. Crimp the crimp bead (Basics) and trim the excess wire.

1 bracelet • Repeat steps 1 to 3 of the necklace. On each end, string a 6 mm pearl and an 8 mm spacer. String alternating 6 mm pearls and 3 mm spacers until the strand is within 2 in. (5 cm) of the finished length.

2 On each end, string a metal accent bead and a 3 mm pearl. Finish as in step 5 of the necklace.

Supplies

Supplies from Eclectica, eclecticabeads.com (click on bead kits).

necklace 15 in. (38 cm)
- ◆ **3** 22 mm charms
- ◆ **2** 13 mm metal accent beads
- ◆ **10** 6 mm glass pearls
- ◆ 16-in. (41 cm) strand 3 mm glass pearls
- ◆ **4** 8 mm spacers
- ◆ **2** 3 mm spacers
- ◆ flexible beading wire, .014 or .015
- ◆ **3** 6 mm jump rings
- ◆ **2** crimp beads
- ◆ toggle clasp
- ◆ chainnose and roundnose pliers, or **2** pairs of chainnose pliers
- ◆ diagonal wire cutters
- ◆ crimping pliers (optional)

bracelet
- ◆ **3** 22 mm charms
- ◆ **2** 13 mm metal accent beads
- ◆ **14–20** 6 mm glass pearls
- ◆ **2** 3 mm glass pearls
- ◆ **6** 8 mm spacers
- ◆ **4–10** 3 mm spacers
- ◆ flexible beading wire, .014 or .015
- ◆ **3** 6 mm jump rings
- ◆ **2** crimp beads
- ◆ toggle clasp
- ◆ chainnose and roundnose pliers, or **2** pairs of chainnose pliers
- ◆ diagonal wire cutters
- ◆ crimping pliers (optional)

earrings
- ◆ **2** 22 mm charms
- ◆ pair of earring wires
- ◆ chainnose and roundnose pliers, or **2** pairs of chainnose pliers

Design alternative

Try substituting round gemstone beads for the glass pearls, and dress up the earrings by adding chain and a few small beads.

earrings • Open the loop of an earring wire (Basics, p. 12). Attach a charm. Close the loop. Make a second earring to match the first.

66These whimsical charms bring back wonderful memories of snorkeling and days at the beach.**99**

Flattering
curves

Double-drilled pearls are key to this
graceful collar-and-earrings set

by Salena Safranski

For a simple, symmetrical necklace, string double-drilled pearls spaced with seed beads. Change the number of seed beads on the bottom strand to create a flattering curve. I chose seed beads that matched the pearls, but you can use contrasting colors for a more dramatic look.

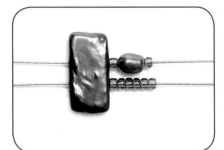

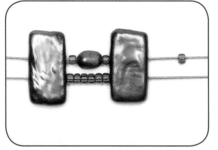

1 **necklace** • Cut a piece of beading wire (Basics, p. 12). Cut a second piece 2 in. (5 cm) longer than the first. Over both wires, string a double-drilled pearl. On the top (short) wire, string an 11º seed bead, a 5 mm pearl, and an 11º. On the bottom wire, string six 11ºs. Repeat the pattern once.

2 Over both wires, string a double-drilled pearl. On the top wire, string an 11º, a 5 mm, and an 11º. On the bottom wire, string seven 11ºs. Over both wires, string a double-drilled pearl. On the top wire, string an 11º, a 5 mm, and an 11º. On the bottom wire, string six 11ºs.
  Repeat step 2 three times.

3 Over both wires, string a double-drilled pearl. On the top wire, string an 11º, a 5 mm, and an 11º. On the bottom wire, string six 11ºs. Over both wires, string a double-drilled pearl. Center the beads.
  On each end of the top wire, string an 11º.

4 On each end of the top wire, string a 5 mm and five 11ºs, repeating the pattern until the strand is within 1 in. (2.5 cm) of the finished length. On each end of the bottom wire, string 11ºs until the strand is within 1 in. (2.5 cm) of the finished length.

5 On each end of each wire, string two 8º seed beads, a crimp bead, an 8º, and the corresponding loop of half of a clasp. Check the fit, and add or remove beads if necessary. Go back through the beads just strung and tighten the wires. Make folded crimps (Basics) and trim the excess wire.

6 Use chainnose pliers to close a crimp cover over each crimp.

" I prefer beading or quilting when I'm with other people, mainly because I like instant feedback. "

229

1 earrings • On a head pin, string a 5 mm pearl. Make the first half of a wrapped loop (Basics, p. 12).

2 Cut two 4-in. (10 cm) pieces of wire.

On one wire, string a double-drilled pearl and make a set of wraps above the bead (Basics). String an 11º seed bead and make a wrapped loop. Repeat with the pearl's remaining hole.

3 Attach the 5 mm unit's loop to a loop of the double-drilled-pearl unit. Complete the wraps.

Open the loop of an earring wire (Basics). Attach the dangle and close the loop. Make a second earring to match the first.

Design alternative

To get more out of the double-drilled pearl strand, make a bracelet. I strung crystals instead of 5 mm pearls on the top and bottom strands.

Tip

The 16-in. (41 cm) pearl strands are enough for two necklaces and two pairs of earrings, so make an extra set for a friend.

Supplies

necklace 16 in. (41 cm)
- ◆ 16-in. (41 cm) strand 15 mm pearls, double drilled
- ◆ 16-in. (41 cm) strand 5 mm pearls
- ◆ **12** 8º seed beads
- ◆ 3 g 11º seed beads
- ◆ flexible beading wire, .014 or .015
- ◆ **4** crimp beads
- ◆ **4** crimp covers
- ◆ two-strand slide clasp
- ◆ chainnose and crimping pliers
- ◆ diagonal wire cutters

earrings
- ◆ **2** 15 mm pearls, double drilled
- ◆ **2** 5 mm pearls
- ◆ **4** 11º seed beads
- ◆ 16 in. (41 cm) 24-gauge half-hard wire
- ◆ **2** 1½-in. (3.8 cm) head pins
- ◆ pair of earring wires
- ◆ chainnose and roundnose pliers
- ◆ diagonal wire cutters

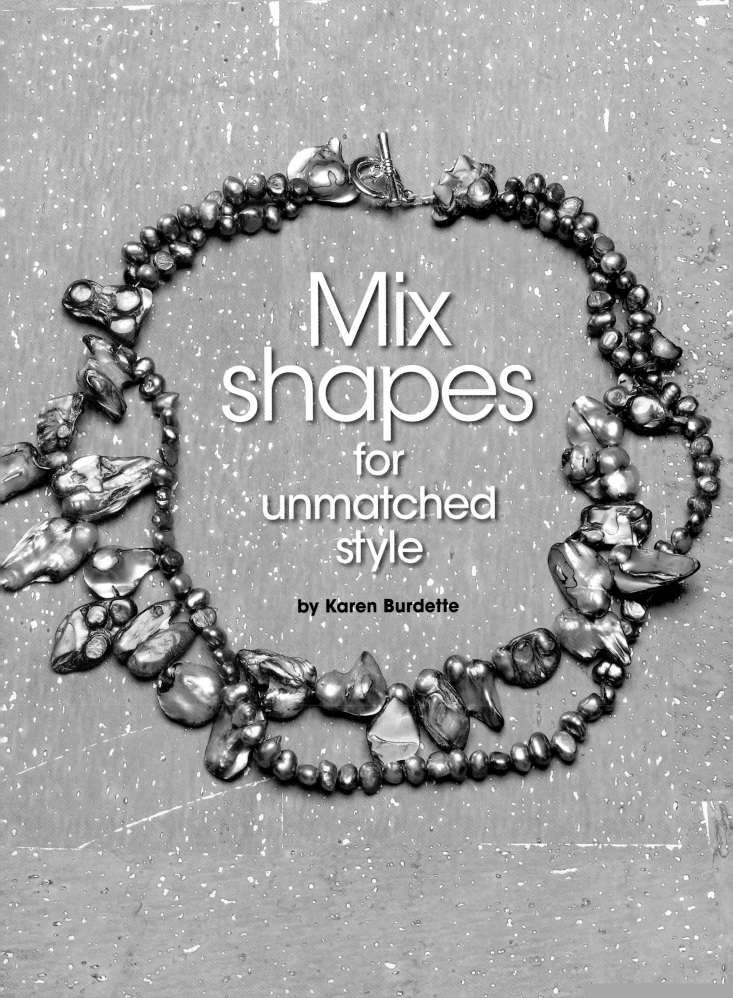

Mix shapes

for unmatched style

by Karen Burdette

Blister and potato pearls create intriguing contrast

My inspiration for jewelry usually comes from the beads themselves. When I saw these pearls at the *Bead&Button* Show last year, I knew they could be combined for a great necklace. The unpredictable jagged shape of the blister pearls really sets off the more traditional pearl strand. The visual chemistry is equally eye-catching in a quick pair of earrings.

1 necklace • Cut two pieces of beading wire (Basics, p. 12). On one wire, string 10 in. (25 cm) of blister pearls.

2 On the second wire, string 12 in. (30 cm) of potato pearls.

3 On each end, over both wires, string a blister pearl. On each end, on each wire, string 2½ in. (6.4 cm) of potato pearls. Allowing 2 in. (5 cm) for finishing, check the fit and add or remove beads from each end if necessary.

4 On each end, over both wires, string a blister pearl, a crimp bead, and half of a clasp. (If the holes of the blister pearls are too small to go back through, string a spacer bead between the pearls and the crimp bead.) Go back through the beads just strung and tighten the wires. Crimp the crimp bead (Basics) and trim the excess wire.

"My start came after I attended the 2005 *Bead&Button* Show and purchased some beads and materials. I made a simple bracelet and was hooked."

Supplies

necklace 17 in. (43 cm)
- 16-in. (41 cm) strand 12–18 mm blister pearls
- **2** 16-in. (41 cm) strands 8 mm potato pearls
- **2** 5 mm round spacer beads (optional)
- flexible beading wire, .010 or .012
- **2** crimp beads
- toggle clasp
- chainnose or crimping pliers
- diagonal wire cutters

earrings
- **2** 12–18 mm blister pearls
- **6** 8 mm potato pearls
- 1½ in. (3.8 cm) cable chain, 2 mm links
- **4** 1½-in. (3.8 cm) head pins
- pair of earring wires
- chainnose and roundnose pliers
- diagonal wire cutters

1 earrings • On a head pin, string a potato pearl, a blister pearl, and a potato pearl. Make a wrapped loop (Basics, p. 12).

2 On a head pin, string a potato pearl. Make the first half of a wrapped loop. Cut a ¾-in. (1.9 cm) piece of chain. Attach the potato-pearl unit. Complete the wraps.

Tip

Before stringing the blister-pearl strand, choose the blister pearls for the earrings and the points where the wires join in the necklace. Look for pairs of pearls with similar shapes.

3 Open the loop of an earring wire (Basics). Attach both dangles. Close the loop. Make a second earring to match the first.

Design alternative

Use boldly dyed shell beads for a brighter, more casual look.

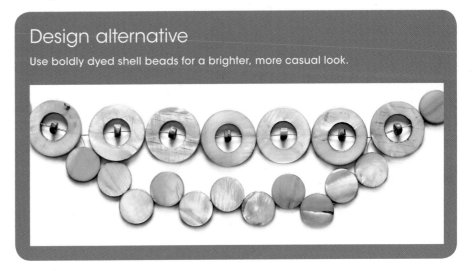

Versatile lariat

A pearl shortener goes the distance to accommodate your style

by Rupa Balachandar

By finishing a strand of beads with a pearl shortener, you'll create multiple style options. Clasp the necklace a few beads from the end so the dangle highlights your décolletage. Or for a classic necklace, clasp the strand close to the end. I like metal spacers between the pearls, but you can also use tiny seed beads, which make the strand look as if it's knotted.

Supplies

Supplies from Rupa B. Designs, rupab.com.

lariat 21 in. (53 cm)
- 24 mm egg pendant
- 16-in. (41 cm) strand 9–10 mm pearls
- **35–41** 3 mm round spacers
- flexible beading wire, .014 or .015
- 9 mm pearl shortener
- **2** crimp beads
- chainnose or crimping pliers
- diagonal wire cutters

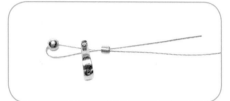

1 Cut a piece of beading wire (Basics, p. 12). String a crimp bead, a pearl shortener, and a spacer. Go back through the shortener and the crimp bead and tighten the wire.

2 Crimp the crimp bead (Basics) and trim the excess wire.

3 String a pearl and a spacer. Repeat until the strand is the finished length, ending with a pearl.

4 String a crimp bead, a spacer, and a pendant. Check the fit, and add or remove beads if necessary. Go back through the last few beads strung and tighten the wire. Crimp the crimp bead and trim the excess wire.

Design alternative

For an organic version, try a lariat with keshi pearls and a Hill Tribe silver pendant.

Tip

Your lariat will be more versatile if it's longer, but check the fit often as you string to find a length that suits you.

Small touches
add charm to a simple set

Petal bead caps give a floral effect to a classic look • by Irina Miech

The sterling silver buds strung on this necklace, bracelet, and earrings are elegant accents to a quick and easy project that will be a wardrobe perennial — or a great gift.

1 necklace · Cut a piece of beading wire (Basics, p. 12). On the wire, center 11 pearls.

2 On each end, string a bead cap.

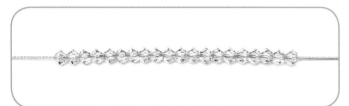

3 On each end, string 3 mm bicone crystals until the necklace is within 1 in. (2.5 cm) of the finished length.

4 On one end, string a crimp bead and a hook clasp. On the other end, string a crimp bead and a 2-in. (5 cm) piece of chain. Check the fit, and add or remove beads from each end if necessary. Go back through the last few beads strung and tighten the wire. Crimp the crimp beads (Basics) and trim the excess wire.

Supplies

All supplies from Eclectica, eclecticabeads.com (click on bead kits).

necklace 15 in. (38 cm)
- ◆ **12** 10 mm glass pearls
- ◆ **105–115** 3 mm bicone crystals
- ◆ **2** 12 mm petal bead caps
- ◆ flexible beading wire, .014 or .015
- ◆ 1½-in. (3.8 cm) head pin
- ◆ **2** crimp beads
- ◆ hook clasp
- ◆ 2 in. (5 cm) cable chain for extender, 4–6 mm links
- ◆ chainnose and roundnose pliers
- ◆ diagonal wire cutters
- ◆ crimping pliers (optional)

bracelet
- ◆ **19–23** 10 mm glass pearls
- ◆ **2** 3 mm bicone crystals
- ◆ **2** 12 mm petal bead caps
- ◆ flexible beading wire, .014 or .015
- ◆ **2** crimp beads
- ◆ toggle clasp
- ◆ chainnose or crimping pliers
- ◆ diagonal wire cutters

earrings
- ◆ **2** 10 mm glass pearls
- ◆ **2** 3 mm bicone crystals
- ◆ **2** 12 mm petal bead caps
- ◆ 4 in. (10 cm) cable chain, 4–6 mm links
- ◆ **2** 1½-in. (3.8 cm) head pins
- ◆ pair of earring wires
- ◆ chainnose and roundnose pliers
- ◆ diagonal wire cutters

5 On a head pin, string a pearl and a bicone. Make the first half of a wrapped loop (Basics).

6 Attach the pearl unit to the chain. Complete the wraps.

bracelet · Follow step 1 of the necklace, stringing pearls until the strand is within 1½ in. (3.8 cm) of the finished length. On each end, string a bead cap, a 3 mm bicone crystal, a crimp bead, and half of a clasp. Check the fit, and add or remove beads if necessary. Go back through the last few beads strung and tighten the wire. Crimp the crimp bead (Basics, p. 12) and trim the excess wire.

Tip

One 16-in. (41 cm) strand of pearls is enough for a necklace, bracelet, and earrings.

1 earrings · On a head pin, string a pearl, a bead cap, and a 3 mm bicone crystal. Make the first half of a wrapped loop (Basics, p. 12).

2 Cut a 2-in. (5 cm) piece of chain. Open the loop of an earring wire (Basics) and attach one end of the chain. Close the loop. Attach the pearl unit to the other end of the chain and complete the wraps. Make a second earring to match the first.

Coin pearls and chain –
a lovely combination

by Rupa Balachandar

Suspend coin pearls from chain in an appealing necklace and earrings

Attach coin pearls to chain for this simple tricolored Y-necklace. If you can't see shelling out for three strands of coin pearls, look for a multicolored strand. Get the most out of your investment by making earrings to match.

1 necklace · On a decorative head pin, string: spacer, color A bicone crystal, color A coin pearl, color A bicone, spacer. Make a wrapped loop (Basics, p. 12).

2 Cut nine 3-in. (7.6 cm) pieces of wire. On one end of one wire, make the first half of a wrapped loop. Attach the bead unit and complete the wraps.
String: spacer, color B bicone, color B pearl, color B bicone, spacer. Make a wrapped loop.

3 On one end of another wire, make the first half of a wrapped loop. Attach the dangle and complete the wraps.
String: spacer, color C bicone, color C pearl, color C bicone, spacer. Make the first half of a wrapped loop.

4 Attach the dangle to the small loop of the loop half of a toggle clasp. Complete the wraps.

On one end of each of two wires, make the first half of a wrapped loop. Attach each to the loop half of the clasp, and complete the wraps.

5 On each wire, string a color A pearl and a color A bicone. Make a wrapped loop.

6 On one end of each of two wires, make the first half of a wrapped loop. Attach a loop and complete the wraps.

On each, string a color B pearl and a color B bicone. Make a wrapped loop.

7 On one end of each of two wires, make the first half of a wrapped loop. Attach a loop and complete the wraps.

   On each wire, string a color C pearl and a color C bicone. Make a wrapped loop.

8 Decide how long you want your necklace to be. Subtract 7 in. (18 cm) and cut a piece of chain to that length. Cut the chain in half. Open two jump rings (Basics) and attach a chain to each wrapped loop. Close the jump rings.

   Check the fit, and trim chain from each end if necessary. Use a jump ring to attach half of a clasp to each chain end.

Supplies

necklace 28 in. (71 cm)
- ◆ **9** 10–12 mm coin pearls, **3** color A, **3** color B, **3** color C
- ◆ **12** 4–5 mm bicone crystals, **4** color A, **4** color B, **4** color C
- ◆ **6** 3 mm round spacers
- ◆ 27 in. (69 cm) 24-gauge half-hard wire
- ◆ 15–25 in. (38–64 cm) chain, 4–5 mm links
- ◆ 2-in. (5 cm) decorative head pin
- ◆ **4** 4 mm jump rings
- ◆ 8–10 mm toggle clasp and additional loop half of a toggle clasp
- ◆ chainnose and roundnose pliers
- ◆ diagonal wire cutters

earrings
- ◆ **4** 10–12 mm coin pearls, **2** color A, **2** color B
- ◆ **4** 4–5 mm bicone crystals, **2** color A, **2** color B
- ◆ 11 in. (28 cm) chain, 4–5 mm links
- ◆ **4** 2-in. (5 cm) head pins
- ◆ **2** 4 mm jump rings
- ◆ pair of lever-back earring wires
- ◆ chainnose and roundnose pliers
- ◆ diagonal wire cutters

1 earrings · On a head pin, string a color A bicone crystal and a color A coin pearl. Make a plain loop (Basics, p. 12). Repeat with a color B pearl and a color B bicone.

2 Cut two pieces of chain, one 2¼ in. (5.7 cm) and one 2¾ in. (7 cm).

   Open the loop of a bead unit (Basics). Attach a chain and close the loop. Repeat with the remaining bead unit and chain.

3 Open a jump ring (Basics) and attach each chain and the loop of an earring wire. Close the jump ring. Make a second earring to match the first.

Pearls

242

night out

Dress up with a pearl choker and earrings

by Roxie Moede

For a choker that's ready to hit the town, start with a favorite button and add pearls. Or start with pearls and then hunt for the perfect centerpiece. If you prefer the second option, try your local craft or sewing store for a broad button selection. Then, string this easy, symmetrical jewelry set to make a striking impression.

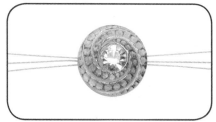

1 necklace • Cut three pieces of beading wire (Basics, p. 12). Over all three wires, center a button.

2 On each end of each wire, string 12 pearls and the corresponding hole of a three-strand spacer bar. Repeat twice. If necessary, string additional pearls until the necklace is within 1 in. (2.5 cm) of the finished length.

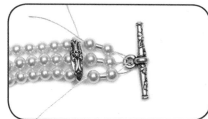

3 On each end of each wire, string a pearl, a crimp bead, and a pearl. On each side, over all three wires, string half of a clasp. Check the fit, and add or remove beads from each end if necessary. Go back through the last few beads strung and tighten the wires. Crimp the crimp beads (Basics) and trim the excess wire.

> **"**I usually have the TV on when I'm beading, mostly for the background noise. I love anything on the Lifetime channel.**"**

1 earrings • On a head pin, string: pearl, spacer, pearl, spacer, pearl. Make a plain loop (Basics, p. 12).

2 Open the loop of an earring wire (Basics). Attach the dangle and close the loop. Make a second earring to match the first.

Design alternative

Make a cuff bracelet with 5 or 6 mm pearls. I strung a five-strand cuff as a variation on the triple-strand choker.

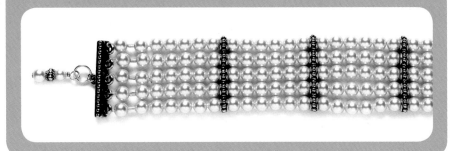

Tip

For a choker that lies just right, use Swarovski crystal pearls. Because they're artificial, the pearls are a uniform size.

Supplies

necklace 13½ in. (34.3 cm)
- 18–23 mm button with shank
- **3** 16-in. (41 cm) strands 4 mm round pearls
- **6** 14–16 mm three-strand spacer bars
- flexible beading wire, .014 or .015
- **6** crimp beads
- toggle clasp
- chainnose or crimping pliers
- diagonal wire cutters

earrings
- **6** 4 mm round pearls
- **4** 4–5 mm flat spacers
- **2** 1½-in. (3.8 cm) head pins
- pair of earring wires
- chainnose and roundnose pliers
- diagonal wire cutters

Arrange a gorgeous palette of glass
and pearls in a monochromatic
necklace and earrings

by Irina Miech

Fluttering
leaves

To make a lush pendant, accent glass leaves and donuts with sparkly crystals. Add a few pearls, and this pendant hangs beautifully. The simple setting and pearl drop earrings add to the classic appeal of this timeless jewelry.

66 Nature is the inspiration for most of my designs. Every walk or bike ride in the park results in bringing home leaves, pods, and seeds. 99

1 necklace • On a 2-in. (5 cm) head pin, string a bicone crystal, a leaf bead, and a bicone. Make the first half of a wrapped loop (Basics, p. 12). Make three leaf units.

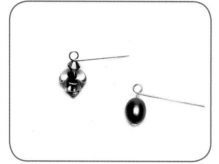

2 On a 1½-in. (3.8 cm) head pin, string a bicone, a donut bead, and a bicone. Make the first half of a wrapped loop. On a second 1½-in. (3.8 cm) head pin, string a pearl. Make the first half of a wrapped loop. Make a total of four or five donut units and four or five pearl units.

3 Cut a 1½-in. (3.8 cm) piece of chain. Attach a leaf unit to the bottom link and complete the wraps.

4 Set aside one pearl unit for step 8. Attach the remaining leaf, donut, and pearl units to the chain as desired, completing the wraps as you go.

5 Cut a piece of beading wire (Basics) and center the pendant.

6 On each end, string pearls until the strand is within 1 in. (2.5 cm) of the finished length.

7 On one end, string a spacer, a crimp bead, a spacer, and a clasp. Repeat on the other end, substituting a 2-in. (5 cm) piece of chain for the clasp. Check the fit, and add or remove beads if necessary. Go back through the beads just strung and tighten the wire. Crimp the crimp beads (Basics) and trim the excess wire.

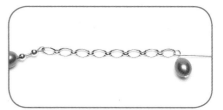

8 Attach a pearl unit to the end link of chain and complete the wraps.

1 earrings • On a head pin, string a pearl and a bicone crystal. Make a wrapped loop (Basics, p. 12).

2 Open the loop of an earring wire (Basics). Attach the bead unit and close the loop. Make a second earring to match the first.

Design alternative

For a simple variation on the leaf theme, string a vermeil or Hill Tribes silver leaf pendant and top-drilled pearls.

Supplies

necklace 15½ in. (39.4 cm)
- **3** 18 mm leaf beads
- **4 or 5** 8 mm donut beads
- 16-in. (41 cm) strand 8 mm pearls
- **14–16** 4 mm bicone crystals
- **4** 3 mm round spacers
- 3½ in. (8.9 cm) chain, 5–6 mm links
- flexible beading wire, .014 or .015
- **3** 2-in. (5 cm) head pins
- **8–10** 1½-in. (3.8 cm) head pins
- **2** crimp beads
- lobster claw clasp

- chainnose and roundnose pliers
- diagonal wire cutters
- crimping pliers (optional)

earrings
- **2** 8 mm pearls
- **2** 4 mm bicone crystals
- **2** 1½-in. (3.8 cm) head pins
- pair of earring wires
- chainnose and roundnose pliers
- diagonal wire cutters

Turn out
a bangle
in no time

by Monica Han

Coiled pearl cuff

Make a spectacular spiral bracelet using just a few materials. The
key piece of equipment is an ingenious rod-and-crank contraption
that makes it easy to quickly coil wire. I used a Coiling Gizmo with a
3 mm-diameter rod for the gold bracelet and a Twist 'n' Curl with a 2 mm
rod for the pink bracelet. The basic model of either product retails for about
$20, but you can also substitute a knitting needle if you prefer a cheaper option.

Supplies

- **2** 10 mm round pearls
- **2–3** 16-in. (41 cm) strands 4 mm round Swarovski pearls
- 2 g 11º or 13º seed beads in a color to match the pearls (optional)
- 22-gauge Artistic Wire (artisticwire.com)
- flexible beading wire, .014 or .015
- **2** crimp beads
- magnetic clasp
- chainnose or crimping pliers
- diagonal wire cutters
- Coiling Gizmo with 3 mm-diameter rod (coilinggizmo.com), Twist 'n' Curl with 2 mm-diameter rod (twistncurl.com), or knitting needle

1 Unwind Artistic Wire from a spool, but do not cut it. String 180 to 220 4 mm pearls.

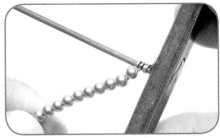

2 String the unbeaded wire through the handle of a rod and bend it to anchor it. Holding the strand firmly, turn the handle to wrap the wire three or four times.

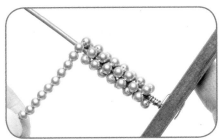

3 Continue turning the handle, wrapping the beaded strand around the rod, until the coiled strand is within 2 in. (5 cm) of the finished length. Make sure there are no gaps in the wire.

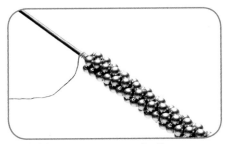

4 Add or remove pearls, if necessary. (If you need to cut wire from the spool, leave a 4-in./ 10 cm tail, to make wrapping easier.) Make three or four plain wire wraps. Remove the coiled strand, and trim the excess wire.

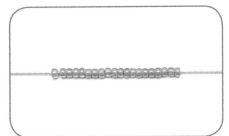

5 Cut a piece of beading wire (Basics, p. 12) and tape one end. String the wire through the coiled strand. If you used a 2 mm-diameter rod, go to step 6. If desired, string seed beads to fill the length of the pearl section.

6 On each end, string a 10 mm pearl, a crimp bead, a 4 mm pearl, and half of a clasp. Check the fit, and add or remove beads if necessary. Go back through the beads just strung and tighten the wire. Crimp the crimp bead (Basics) and trim the excess wire.

Tips

- Try Artistic Wire in a shade to match the pearls.
- Each 16-in. (41 cm) strand of 4 mm round Swarovski pearls has 100 pearls. I needed only two strands for the pink bracelet. I used three strands for the gold bracelet, which is slightly longer and has a wider diameter. To estimate how many you'll need, figure about 37 pearls per inch for a wider bracelet.

Shortcuts
Readers' tips to make your beading life easier

rake rack
I made a jewelry rack with the metal head of a garden rake. I removed the head from the handle, cleaned and painted it, and decorated it with artificial flowers. The curved tines are long enough to hold many necklaces and bracelets.

– Barbara McAleese, Yuma, AZ

earring display
I display earrings on my business cards. Then I put them in plastic bags to keep them neat and secure. I tack the bags to a cork board for display on an easel at craft shows. I can fit 50 pairs of earrings on a 15 x 21-in. (38 x 53 cm) board.

– Olivia Wendorf, Charlotte, MI

digital design tool
My digital camera is an indispensable jewelry-creation tool. I take photos of beads to see how different colors and shapes work together. I also take photos of pieces that don't seem to be working so I can better see how to fix them. Finally, when I get an idea that makes me want to change course in the middle of a project, I take a photo before I undo any work. Knowing I can go back to the earlier version frees me to take creative risks.

– Michelle Mach, via e-mail

nonsticky glue tubes
Use a lotion-infused tissue to wipe the tip of a glue tube before closing it. The lotion keeps the cap from sticking.

– Chris Thommen, Portage, MI

left-handed complement
When making a necklace with a one-sided pendant for a left-handed friend, attach the business end of the clasp to the left side of the necklace so it will be on your friend's left side when she wears it.

– Sandra Porter, Vancouver, WA

foam ear guards
Use a hole punch and craft foam to make easy, economical ear guards for French earring wires. Use a sharp pin to make a hole in the center of the foam circle before putting it on the earring.

– Nicole Jeske, Minocqua, WI

anti-tarnish storage

For an easy and inexpensive way to store jewelry between shows, I roll it in anti-tarnish cloth. The jewelry doesn't get tangled and the cloth helps prevent tarnish. One yard cut in half lengthwise will make two rolls. For additional tarnish protection, store the rolls in sealed plastic containers with anti-tarnish strips. The cloth is available at most fabric stores.

– *Becky Malone, Westminster, CO*

bead organizer

A Stanley Tool Organizer (model 14166 is shown) is a handy way to store and transport beads. You can adjust the size of the compartments, and the side drawers are great for strung beads and finished pieces.

– *Judi Case, Long Valley, NJ*

fluted pans

When I'm working with smaller beads that come in tubes or small packages, I pour them into metal tartlet pans with fluted edges. The fluted edges act like funnels for pouring the beads back into their containers.

– *Cheryl Wilson, Blaine, MN*

corduroy work surface

Instead of throwing old corduroy clothes away, I cut them into square pieces to use as work surfaces. The ridges in the fabric are great for lining up beads.

– *Tess Cysz, Lee, MA*

tape and foil

To safely store an unfinished project, stick a long strip of double-sided tape down the center of a piece of foil, place your beads on the tape, and fold the foil.

– *DeLaine L. Fry, via e-mail*

pillbox storage

I use a seven-day pillbox with detachable compartments to store jump rings, earring wires, and crimp beads. It's compact, so I can easily carry my findings with me.

– *Danna Givot, Ramona, CA*

Contributors

Gia Amschel Contact Gia in care of *BeadStyle*.

Rupa Balachandar A world traveler, Rupa creates jewelry that makes a statement. She regularly travels through Asia and is pleased to share her finds through www.rupab.com. Contact her via e-mail at info@rupab.com.

Donna Marie Bates Donna is a business person who realized the creative power inside her when she began working with brilliant design materials. Contact DonnaMarie at dbates5@nycap.rr.com or visit jewelrybydonnamarie.com

Ute Bernsen An artist, silk painter, meditation teacher, and jewelry designer, Ute is creating a course that combines beading or painting with meditation. Contact her at ute@silkpaintingisfun.com

Mary Bloomsburg For Mary, beading is a way to create and relax at the same time. She designs kits and teaches classes in Kennewick, Wash. Contact Mary at admin@Treasurechestbeads.com or visit her Web site, www.Treasurechestbeads.com.

Heather Boardman Heather is an avid lampworker and jewelry designer. She creates glass beads using bright colors and strong shapes. Heather also has a line of "green" beads made out of vintage bottles reclaimed from historic farm properties. Contact her at heather@hmbstudios.com or visit her Web site at hmbstudios.com.

Jackie Boettcher Beading provides a creative outlet for Jackie, who is a credit assistant for Kalmbach Publishing Co. Contact her at jboettcher@kalmbach.com.

Jodi Broehm Jodi's four-year-old hobby quickly became an addiction. "When I see beads that I love, they practically string themselves!" Contact Jodi in care of *BeadStyle*.

Karen Burdette Karen Burdette, a credit specialist, also loves reading. Contact Karen at kburdette@kalmbach.com.

Sarah Caligiuri Sarah loves the primitive elegance of roughly faceted stones and the diversity of wire. She also has a passion for the Wu Li and Native American inspiration. She lives in southern California. Contact her at sarahcreates@yahoo.com or visit sarahcreates.com.

Maria Camera Maria co-owns Bella Bella! in Milwaukee, Wis. with her sister, Christianne. Contact Maria in care of *BeadStyle*.

Jenna Colyar-Cooper Jenna Colyar-Cooper has been beading since she was a little girl. Since graduating with an art history degree from Western Washington University, she has continued to pursue her love of beads. Contact Jenna via e-mail at info@fusionbeads.com.

Carolyn Conley The first time Carolyn saw lampworked beads, she was captivated by their beauty. Now she incorporates them into her own unique jewelry designs. See more beads at beadsbyccdesign.com or contact Carolyn at ccdesign@cableone.net.

Nina Cooper Through her company Nina Designs, Nina uses creativity and innovation to bring inspired beads, findings, and jewelry designs to bead enthusiasts around the world. Reach her at www.ninadesigns.com.

Angie D'Amato Angie's latest collection reflects the vintage glam, feminine, and classy style of the late 1800s and early 1900s. Contact Angie at D'Amato Designs, damatodesigns@internode.on.net or visit damatodesignsjewellry.com.

Miachelle De Piano Miachelle, a technical writer, runs her jewelry business on the side. She has been making jewelry for seven years and is active in the artistic community in Phoenix, Ariz. Contact Miachelle via e-mail at cosmoaccessories@cox.net or visit her Web site, cosmopolitanaccessories.net.

Jessica Fehrman Jessica has dabbled in many varieties of home crafts but is now intrigued with the creativity of beading beautiful jewelry. She has a business for custom special occasion jewelry and a Web site, www.sparklingc.com.

Roxanne Fraga Roxanne's store, Chic Beads, is in Los Alamitos, Calif. One of her more challenging designs was for the Disney character Ariel in celebration of Disneyland's 50th anniversary. Contact Roxanne at roxanne@chicbeads.com or visit her Web site, chicbeads.com.

Naomi Fujimoto Naomi is senior editor for *BeadStyle*.

Sue Godfrey Sue Godfrey's jewelry designs are available in several Wisconsin boutiques. Sue works and teaches at Midwest Beads in Brookfield, Wis. Contact her at highstrungsue@wi.rr.com.

Mia Gofar Mia is a jewelry designer and author from Singapore. Contact her via e-mail at mia@miagofar.com or her Web site at miagofar.com.

Karey Grant Karey's design advice? "Stop thinking and start doing." Contact Karey through her Web site, inspiredbystones.com.

Marla Gulotta Marla Gulotta's passion for jewelry began after years of collecting vintage jewelry, leading her into designing new jewelry with an eye to the past. She can be reached at attolug@sbcglobal.net.

Lauren M. Hadley Lauren is inspired by the contour, color, and texture of the materials she uses. View her work at her etsy shop at mariemarie.etsy.com or contact her by e-mail at mariemarie103@aol.com.

Astrid Hall Astrid's world revolves around style and color. Her early European travels inspired her; her experience was further enhanced with engineering prep school and being the general manager of a high-couture skirt factory. Contact Astrid at gems2behold@gems2behold.com or visit gems2behold.com.

Monica Han Monica is an award-winning mixed-media jewelry designer and teacher from Potomac, Md. Contact her at mhan@dreambeads.biz.

Linda Arline Hartung Linda is an avid jewelry designer and teacher. Her designs and techniques are featured in jewelry-making publications worldwide. Contact her via e-mail at linda@alacarteclasps.com, or visit her Web sites, alacarteclasps.com or wirelace.com.

Cathy Jakicic is editor of *BeadStyle*.

Steven James Armed with his mantra, "What are you gonna make today?," Steven blends beads and jewelry making into home décor and everyday living. Visit his Web site, macaroniandglitter.com.

Louise Jeremich Based in New Jersey, Louise specializes in one-of-a-kind and limited edition pieces. Contact her at JeremichDesigns@aol.com or view her work at AllBentOuttaShape.etsy.com.

Lisa Kan Bead and lampwork artist Lisa Kan is inspired by nature, ceramics, Japanese arts, and Victorian-era jewelry. She's an avid researcher and enjoys sharing the art and craft of beading through her writings. Contact Lisa at lisakandesigns@yahoo.com or visit lisakan.com.

Carole Kane A lifelong artist, Carole's mother's continuous support led her to an art career, and now Carole teams with her daughter. Contact her at ckane2000@sbc-global.net or visit beadworkbydesign.com.

Eva Kapitany Eva began making jewelry to ease her depression. Her husband said, "Keep doing whatever you're doing, 'cause I've never seen you happier." Eva's been depression-free and designing jewelry for seven years. Contact her in care of *BeadStyle*.

Sue Kennedy Sue makes glass beads in her home studio in Pittsburgh, Pa. To see more of her work, visit her Web site at suebeads.com or contact her at sue@suebeads.com.

Jane Konkel Jane Konkel is associate editor of *BeadStyle*.

Alice Lauber Alice began by exhibiting her jewelry designs at art shows throughout the Midwest. In 1997, she opened Midwest Beads with her husband Gary. She concentrates her efforts on the bead shop and raising four young children. Any spare time is spent on creating new jewelry designs. Alice can be reached at Midwest Beads, midwestbeads@sbcglobal.net.

Monica Lueder Jewelry designer Monica Lueder enjoys adding an elegant flair to her designs. She can be reached at mdesign@wi.rr.com.

Gretchen McHale An event planner in Philadelphia, Pa., Gretchen has come a long way from when she raided her dad's fishing box for jewelry making supplies. Contact her at gretchmcha@aol.com.

Carol McKinney What happens when an interior designer turns to jewelry design? She creates unique, one-of-a-kind pieces that take fashion to a new level. Contact Carol McKinney at lemon.leopard@hotmail.com or through her Web site, lemonleopard.com.

Kerry Melson Voted "most likely to own a jewelry store" in high school, Kerry Melson makes lampworked beads in addition to designing and making jewelry. Contact Kerry at rust567@aol.com, or visit her Web site, theresaspromise.com.

Irina Miech Irina is an artist, teacher, and the author of a series of popular how-to books on metal-clay and wirework jewelry design for beaders. She also oversees a 6,000-square-foot retail bead supply business and classroom studio. Contact Irina at eclecticainfo@sbcglobal.net.

Roxie Moede Roxie Moede's favorite place to bead is with her cat sleeping next to her. Contact Roxie at rmoede@kalmbach.com.

Joanna Mueller Joanna Mueller has been a glass bead and jewelry maker for several years. Although detailed design inspires her, she's always trying new and simple things. Contact Joanna Mueller via e-mail at sleekbeads@yahoo.com or her Web site at sleekbeads.com.

Jennifer Ortiz Observing the clothing color combinations of others inspires Jennifer's beading designs. Contact her at jenortiz794@yahoo.com.

Ali Otterbein Ali is only 15 but has been surrounded by beads her entire life. Living above a bead store gives her lots to choose from, but as she puts it, "You can be just as creative using your stash of leftover beads." Contact Ali via e-mail at kimodesign@msn.com.

Paula Radke Paula has been creating art glass for almost 25 years. She has a deep love of bright colors and shiny things, which explains her passion for dichroic glass. Contact Paula at info@paularadke.com or visit paularadke.com.

Melissa Rediger Melissa is a stay-at-home mother to four little children. She's a self-taught lampwork artist who's been making glass beads for eight years. Reach her at rediger@netins.net and see her beads and jewelry online at www.mjrbeads.com.

Betty Rodriguez Betty attributes her passion for color and art to her Latino heritage. She markets her jewelry at craft shows and online at www.earringsbybetty.etsy.com. Contact Betty at laredorosegems@yahoo.com.

Salena Safranski Salena feels most creative when she's listening to old jazz and drinking coffee. Her inspiration for the double-drilled pearl necklace? A latte. Contact Salena in care of *BeadStyle*.

Karla Schafer Karla Schafer is a full-time designer. She's influenced by the power of nature and natural stones. Contact Karla via e-mail at karla@auntiesbeads.com or visit the Web site, auntiebeads.com.

Brenda Schweder The author of *Junk to Jewelry* and *Vintage Redux*, Brenda is a frequent jewelry-magazine contributor. Visit her Web site, brendaschweder.com, or e-mail her at b@brendaschweder.com.

Debbi Simon Debbi paints, teaches, and designs and makes jewelry. She's the author of *Crystal Chic* and a frequent contributor to *BeadStyle*.

Diane Tadlock Contact Diane in care of *BeadStyle*.

Juliana Thaens Beautiful beads provide plenty of inspiration for Juliana. Contact her at julianascreations@yahoo.com or see more work at www.julianascreations.etsy.com.

Gretta Van Someren A hobbyist turned executive, Gretta's passion continues to grow. Her designs have been seen on television, featured in magazines, and worn by celebrities. Contact her at gretta@atterg.com or visit her Web site at www.atterg.com.

Stephanie A. White As a little girl, Stephanie loved beading, and it's no surprise to her family that it became her business. View her designs at her online store, SWCreations Jewelry, contact her at jewelry@swcreations.net or visit www.swcreations.net.

Jean Yates Jean Yates, of Westchester, N.Y., wrote *Links*, a jewelry design book. She specializes in wirework with polymer and lampworked beads. Contact her at prettykittydogmoonjewelry.com or visit prettykittydogmoonjewelry.blogspot.com.

Index

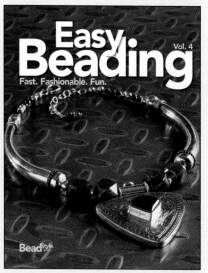